James Drummond

Spiritual Religion

Sermons on Christian Faith and Life

James Drummond

Spiritual Religion
Sermons on Christian Faith and Life

ISBN/EAN: 9783337086008

Printed in Europe, USA, Canada, Australia, Japan

Cover: Foto ©Lupo / pixelio.de

More available books at **www.hansebooks.com**

Sermons

ON

CHRISTIAN FAITH AND LIFE.

BY

JAMES DRUMMOND, B.A.

Χριστῷ συνεσταύρωμαι· ζῶ δὲ οὐκέτι ἐγώ, ζῇ δὲ ἐν ἐμοὶ Χριστός.
ST. PAUL, *Gal.* ii. 20.

LONDON:

LONGMANS, GREEN, AND CO.

1870.

PREFACE.

———◦◦◦———

THIS LITTLE VOLUME is offered to the public as
a very lowly contribution towards the settlement
of some of the great religious questions which are
agitated at the present day. If in these Sermons the
thoughtful reader should miss the completeness and
severity of argument which he might properly
demand in an elaborate treatise, it is hoped that he
will find some compensation in the greater vividness
with which the connection between truth and the
ordinary life of men may be presented in that form
of composition which is intended primarily to
influence the affections and conduct.

To that increasing class of men, who, while pro-
foundly conscious of a spiritual power in Christianity, are yet unable to accept any of the current
representations of it, it is hoped that the thoughts
here presented may not be altogether devoid of
interest and value. They are at least an honest

statement of private conviction, and an endeavour to survey the subjects treated of without the injurious bias of party trammels.

In one point I must crave the indulgence of critics of the New Testament. In referring to the Gospels under the ordinary titles, I do not mean to commit myself to any special theory of their authorship. It did not belong to my plan to discuss that subject, nor are the views here advocated dependent on the doubtful results of a literary investigation. It seemed, therefore, simplest to adopt the usual mode of reference.

To the Congregation to which it has been my privilege to minister for several years, this volume may probably express more than to the general reader. To its members I would dedicate it, as a tribute of grateful affection, in the hope that it may, in some slight degree, help to preserve among them that combined life of spiritual devotedness and intellectual freedom which they have inherited, and of which I trust some traces will be found in the Sermons which are now offered to their acceptance.

HAMPSTEAD :
February 2, 1870.

CONTENTS.

a

SPIRITUAL RELIGION.

THE CHRISTIAN'S DISTINCTIVE FAITH.—I.

1 Corinthians xii. 3.

' I give you to understand, that no man speaking by the Spirit of God calleth Jesus accursed: and that no man can say that Jesus is the Lord, but by the Holy Spirit.'

At a time when, whatever may be our wishes or tendencies, we cannot but admit that remarkable changes of opinion are taking place, and that men are gradually drifting from their ancient moorings towards some yet undetermined goal, the question— what are the essential features of that Christianity which we in common profess?—cannot fail to awaken our deepest interest. Does the movement which is in progress indicate the approaching consummation of the great Protestant revolt from mediæval super- stition, and our final emergence into the light and freedom of truly spiritual thought and practice? or does it imply, as Roman Catholics maintain, that

B

Protestantism is at last manifesting its natural incoherence, and dissolving itself into chaos, prepara-
tory to our reabsorption into the Roman Church?
Is the incoherence among liberals a source of weakness or of strength?   Is it the expression of a great
principle, or the inevitable looseness of those who
have no principle? the result of a faith which is to
conquer the world, or the feeble offspring of doubt
and self-will?   Upon these questions we ought to
be prepared with an intelligent answer; for we know
not how soon the struggle may be at our doors, how
soon all existing sects may be resolved into two
great parties, the advocates of authority and of freedom, or, as I should rather express it, the advocates
of external and of internal authority, those who uphold the supremacy of the Church and those who
uphold the supremacy of conscience, those who find
God chiefly in others and those who find Him
chiefly in themselves.   This subject might carry me
far beyond the limits of a discourse; and to-day we
must confine ourselves to the preliminary question,
what is the fundamental faith which we hold as
Christians?

This question possesses great importance in many
aspects.   Even those who, while living in the midst
of a Christian civilisation, profess to regard Christianity as one of the effete religions of the past,
ought in fairness to interest themselves in this
inquiry, in order that they may ascertain whether

the religion itself is responsible for those systems
which provoke their hostility. But those to whom
the name Christian is still a word with power, suggestive of all that is noblest and mightiest in human
affairs, ought for many reasons to seek the purest
and most exalted conception of its meaning. Calling
themselves Christians, they ought to know what it
is that they profess, and not lightly and irreverently
borrow their title from Him the latchet of whose
shoes they are not worthy to loose. The view which
we form of the meaning and of the requirements of
Christianity must largely influence our judgment of
ourselves, and give the prevailing tone to our character; and it is at our peril that we adopt false or
superficial views. Our judgment of others also is
dependent upon the solution of the question before
us. Men have been fond of denying the Christian
name to one another. This denial has been used as
a weapon of terrible oppression at a time when,
involved despair in this world, and, as men thought,
eternal torment in the next; and is occasionally used
still, though it is apt to recoil upon the head of the
accuser, and serves chiefly to warn us of the self-
deception of conscientious acrimony. We ought,
however, to be sensitively fearful, lest we should be
unjust in this matter. Although we may maintain,
as has been maintained with a certain show of libe-
rality, that Christianity is only a form of belief,
about which men may reasonably differ, and that

therefore we think no worse of a man for not being a Christian, still it is a very serious thing to refuse the Christian name to any man who claims it; for, in the popular understanding, this refusal carries with it a moral stigma which renders a man liable to suspicion and dislike. We ought to satisfy ourselves on the most solid grounds that such refusal is not only just, but required of us by the imperative voice of duty, before we adopt a measure which may wound a brother's heart, and subject him, so far as our in-fluence extends, to that degree of social obloquy which the manners of the day permit.

There is one other reason, on which we must touch, for examining the present subject. If we value Christianity, we must regard it as of the highest moment to give a true representation of it to those whose hearts it has not yet reached. Whether we bear it to the impure and neglected districts of our own cities, which offer so appalling a comment upon our national religion, or send it across the seas to lands which still lie under the shadow of idolatry and superstition, we ought to be anxious to present it in its essential power, and shrink, as from a thought of blasphemy, from the possibility of ten-dering some poor system of our own instead of the Divine reality. Alas for us, if the blindness of our hearts and our arrogant self-assertion prevent it from winning its way and taking captive the soul with its ancient might, or if the strange dogmas and forms which we dignify with its name cause it to be rejected with indignation and disgust!

When we turn to the sects of Christendom for an answer to our question, we are thrown into some perplexity, not only on account of the variety, but also on account of the obscurity, of the answers. Generally speaking, we have a large body of dogmas, the denial of any one of which is supposed to endanger your Christian standing. Christianity is represented as embracing a complete system of theology and practice, and he who is faulty in his views of any one point is in effect guilty of rejecting the whole. To test our Christianity by one of these systems would require us to go through its articles one by one, and consider in regard to each whether it really commanded our assent; but this process would be too tedious, and might perhaps subject certain dogmas to a scrutiny which they could ill bear; and it is needful, therefore, to seek some comprehensive statement under which the separate points may be included. There are two such statements in that part of Christendom with which we are best acquainted, which represent two diverging lines of thought, and are maintained respectively by the two great divisions of Western Christianity, the Catholic and the Protestant Churches.

If I rightly understand the Catholic position, the prime essential of Christianity is there conceived to be an absolute submission to the authority of the

Roman Catholic Church. This Church is regarded as a permanent miraculous power upon earth, whose voice is the utterance of infallible truth and wisdom, and from whose sentence there is no appeal. This appears to furnish us with a simple point of belief; but the simplicity is delusive. In accepting the authority of the Roman Catholic Church, we implicitly accept all that that Church may teach; and the number of propositions is absolutely appalling, the denial of which renders a man liable to a curse. As an example, on the question of justification alone the Council of Trent has adopted thirty-three canons, of which this is the unvarying form— 'If any man shall think so and so, let him him be accursed.' Many, indeed, of these canons, apart from their curse, appear to me sound and judicious; but when I come to the nine canons relating to the Mass, and the eight relating to Ordination, I find myself in the position of an unbeliever, and liable, in the opinion of the Roman Church, to eternal damnation. It must not be forgotten, therefore, that in acknowledging the supremacy of the Roman Church we should at the same time pledge ourselves to the acceptance of a vast system of dogma, and that, in regard to all the most important theological questions, we should thenceforward abrogate the right of our conscience and reason to be heard, and be forced to shrink from the inquiries suggested by advancing knowledge as from the blight of sin or the cold hand of death. We cannot at present enter into the details of the Catholic scheme of theology. The dogma of the Church's infallibility seems to include all the rest; and to deny this infallibility, either in general, or in relation to particular points, destroys, in the view of this scheme, your title to the Christian name.

In opposition to the infallibility of the Church, another authority has been set up, and very widely recognised among Protestants. The infallibility of the Bible has been assumed as the basis on which must rest the whole superstructure of Christian belief and practice. As General Councils have pronounced their own conclusions to be the immediate declarations of the Holy Spirit, so Protestant theologians have maintained that every line of the Bible is a direct utterance from God. The Westminster Confession of Faith speaks of God as 'the Author' of the Holy Scripture, and of its 'infallible truth and Divine authority.' The doctrine of the Established Church in England is much less explicit; but, when no legal question is involved, I think we may fairly gather from the mode in which reference is made to the Scripture throughout the Articles that the infallibility of the Bible is assumed as the unquestionable basis of all Christian truth, beyond which there is no appeal. This has certainly been the popular view; and, although it has been impossible to establish a legal case against the Bishop of Natal, we all know what a clamour has been raised against him, not on account of his denying any article of religious belief, but on account of his doubting the Mosaic authorship and perfect credibility of the Pentateuch. Now, this dogma of the infallibility of the Scriptures, like that of the infallibility of the Church, seems to possess an attractive simplicity, and to furnish a basis on which Christians might readily unite; but, as in the latter case, the simplicity disappears upon further examination. The dogma carries with it the acceptance of a vast multiplicity of statements, religious, historical, and scientific. In relation to all these statements, the individual conscience and reason must be silent; and however the heart may revolt against the propriety and bliss of dashing your enemy's little ones against the stones, however impossible the intellect may find it to reconcile statements which appear clearly contradictory, you must ascribe your difficulties to your 'carnal' mind, and believe that the light that is in you is darkness. Carried out to its legitimate extent, therefore, the Protestant dogma is just as oppressive as the Romanist; and if this oppression, this laying of the individual mind under the absolute control of an authority external to itself, be an objection to the one system, it is no less an objection to the other; and if it be invalid as an argument against the Protestant position, it is equally invalid against the Catholic. It is difficult, indeed, to see any difference in principle between the two systems, the distinction being simply this, that the one maintains that the Church was infallible from the time of Moses till the death of the last Apostle, while the other holds that the infallibility remains through its entire history.

But what, then, becomes of the Protestant right of private judgment? Originally, I believe, it expressed the conviction that there is in the heart and conscience of man a witness whose authority is greater than any which can come to us from without. The Protestant movement was not, in the first instance, so much a doctrinal revolt, as an assertion that the indelible moral convictions of the human soul had a right to make themselves heard, all decisions of popes and councils to the contrary notwithstanding. But when the infallibility of the Bible became the recognised dogma, and was used as the accepted Protestant symbol to oppose to the Roman claims, the right of private judgment was limited to the right of interpreting the Scriptures. Men who accepted the Bible as the supreme, ultimate authority were permitted to differ as to the teachings of this authority; but to call the authority itself in question, or to suppose that the individual conscience or reason could invalidate even the least of its statements was, and to a large extent is, regarded as infidelity. The liberty of interpretation was not, however, left unrestricted; for in various communities authoritative statements of the meaning of Scripture were issued, and most sects subsided into a hard dogmatic system, where liberty and the right of private judgment remained only as sepulchral echoes from a living world that had been left.

Can either of these positions satisfy us as truly representing the claims of Christianity? Without at present calling in question the truth of the dogmas themselves, there appears to me to be one very serious objection to putting them in the front of the Christian battle, and making the whole cause depend upon their success. They are not dogmas so intrinsically evident, and so appealing to the most sober wisdom and purest instincts of our nature, as to make themselves universally or almost universally acceptable. A large number of thoughtful and conscientious men—and indeed, I think I may say, of those who have really examined these subjects a considerable proportion—have not only doubts as to the soundness of the dogmas, but feel perfectly satisfied that they are not correct. Now, admitting that the view of these men may be erroneous, still we cannot but feel that in such a case there must be considerable uncertainty in the evidence, and that, if Christianity be really bound up with either of these doctrines, its fate is trembling in the balance. It is a sign of ill omen when the clergy, who ought to be the best prepared to meet every legitimate doubt, to sympathise with and clear away the diffi-

culties which are felt even with a sad and regretful
earnestness by so many, and to construct a theology
worthy of the time, are weakly railing at science,
vilifying men who cannot accept the current dogma,
and declaring that all spiritual truth is lost if that one
dogma be impugned. There is danger lest the threat-
ening prophecy may bring its own fulfilment, and
that men, forced by advancing knowledge from their
ancient ground, will find themselves unprepared;
and the shepherds of the people may lament, when
too late, that they have contented themselves with
appealing to prejudice, when they ought to have
thrown themselves with purest and wisest sympathy
and largest culture into the intellectual and spiritual
movements of their age.

If, therefore, there be in Christianity any pearl
of truth or of religious power which is independent
of the infallibility of either Church or Bible, and
rests upon a surer basis, it is of the highest consequence that this should be found, and pressed
earnestly upon the attention of those who, in sorrow
or in disgust, are forsaking the systems of the past. To
discover this pearl is the object of liberal theologians,
those 'unhappy' men so obnoxious to the hatred
of ecclesiastics, and all the more disliked because
the ecclesiastical mind cannot comprehend them.
They are a strange, incoherent set, disowning all
party ties—vowing eternal allegiance, not to opinions,
but to truth,—listening, not to the watch-word of sect

or Church, but to the awful voice of God in their own
souls.   Feeble, disconnected atoms, must they not
soon be swallowed up—these men who flaunt no
banner, and do not fear to be alone?   Shifting to
and fro, and presenting no completed system, what
can they do against the mighty phalanx of Roman
dogma, or the thirty-nine standards that lift themselves so proudly above the hosts of English thought?
Strange sound to a sectarian world, their lonely
freedom constitutes the very majesty of power.
Galileo was the mouthpiece of no party, and offered
no completed scheme of science; yet his word has
not died, and shall not die, and the thunders of
ecclesiastical rebuke have recoiled helpless from that
solitary man.   And a greater than Galileo dared to
stand aloof from parties, and to speak in simplicity
from the fulness of his own soul.   Priests were
strong enough to crucify him; but their ecclesiastical
polity, which boasted to have its foundation upon the
Rock of Ages, has come to nought, and He stands
above the world peerless and alone.   And now, if
they are content to bear their cross, and can disdain
the charm of party sympathies and unalterable
systems of thought, these men who, for want of a
better name, may be called liberals in religion, will
surely triumph.   Only in freedom can the soul
attain its highest power; and the dense battalions
of error will silently melt away before the subtile
attacks of viewless and unshackled truth.   There is

no logical resting-place between absolute submission
to external authority and absolute liberty to use, as
best we can, the faculties which God has given us.
To this great issue all our controversies are tending.
Is Christianity, then, to perish? or is Christ the
harbinger of liberty, and will the emancipated world
still shout hosannas in honour of his name? This
question must be postponed to another occasion;
but meanwhile we may find much food for reflection
upon this subject in the words of the text, into the
immediate consideration of which I have been unable
to enter:—' No man speaking by the Spirit of God
calleth Jesus accursed: and no man can say that
Jesus is the Lord, but by the Holy Spirit.'

II.

THE CHRISTIAN'S DISTINCTIVE FAITH.—II.

1 CORINTHIANS xii. 3.

'*I give you to understand, that no man speaking by the Spirit of God calleth Jesus accursed: and that no man can say that Jesus is the Lord, but by the Holy Spirit.*'

IN my last discourse I briefly noticed some of the views which have been held in later times as to the fundamental faith of Christianity; to-day we have to return to the earliest records of the religion, and consider what may be learned upon this subject from the pages of the New Testament.

To any inquiry of this kind it has been objected that it is absurd to suppose that Christianity can be anything different from what it has always been represented to be, that the great mass of professing Christians must be the true exponents of its doctrines, and that the little heretical sects which have been flung off from the main body, as no longer participating in its essential life, have no title to be heard in the matter. Now, if we were not in possession of early documents, this might appear a reasonable and valid argument; but holding, as we

do, a series of writings which have preserved for us
the first impression which Christianity made upon
the world, we naturally turn to them to ascertain
the distinguishing features of the religion. We
ought not, indeed, in fairness to expect an elaborately constructed scheme of Christian theology in
the few writings which have remained to us from
the first age, and we cannot but admit that doctrines
may have taken shape in later times which truly
embodied Christian belief, and had previously been
enfolded, as it were, in its original ideas, and were
therefore required for its complete expression. But
we may surely look for the great fundamental principles of the religion, which made the deepest impression upon men's minds, and formed the bond of
union among the first believers ; and we may justly
regard these principles as the ground-work of
Christian theology, and apply them as a test to the
doctrines of a later age. Let us endeavour, then,
to lay aside all previous conceptions which may
bias our inquiry, and to ascertain from the New
Testament itself the distinctive feature of Christianity.

First, however, let us see that we understand
clearly the problem which is before us. We are
not seeking for all those truths which are contained in
Christianity, and which, in some respects, may
appear to be incomparably its most important parts.
There are some grand moral principles, such as the

obligation of justice and purity, some profound and comprehensive religious doctrines, such as those which affirm the existence of one spiritual God and the reality of a future life, which are common to it with other forms of religion, and which, however essential to the Christian, do not in any way distinguish him from those who call themselves by a different name.   But we are now in search of that which is the distinctive mark of Christianity, and separates it from other forms of religion ; for that which so colours and vivifies the universal principles of religion and morality as to give them a peculiarly Christian aspect ; for that which at the first preaching of the Gospel flooded these principles with a new power, and carried them home triumphantly to the hearts of men.   To take an illustration, if we were inquiring into the characteristics of any particular tribe of men, we would disregard all the common human features, though these would undoubtedly constitute their highest honour, and we would fix our attention solely upon what was special to themselves, such as an unusual fineness of intellect or an unexampled sensibility to religious impressions.   So in the case before us, let it be understood that we are seeking, not necessarily for the most important, but for the *distinctive* feature of Christianity.

The first thing that strikes us on turning to the New Testament is the total absence of all formal definitions which might serve to settle our question.

The very terms in which we state our question are not to be found. The word 'Christianity' does not occur, nor is there any other recognised name for the new religion. The word 'Christian' is indeed used, but only three times; and then in such connections as to suggest that it was the name given, probably in contempt, by others rather than adopted by the Christians themselves; and it is not once met with in the writings of Paul and John, which form the most doctrinal portion of the New Testament. A term by which the Christians are frequently described is 'disciples,' a word which represents them simply as men who looked to Christ as their teacher; but this term occurs only in the Gospels and the Book of Acts. The names which are generally applied to them are 'Brothers'—a word expressive of mutual love, and by no means limited to professed Christians — and 'Saints,' or holy ones, a name denoting consecration to a divine life. Equally remarkable is the want of any creed, or formal statement of the belief which was avowed by Christians; of tests to be offered to converts, or enforced against heretics; and of rules to regulate the affairs of the new society. The association which founded the Church of the future, eighteen centuries ago, being little versed in the arts of modern civilisation, did not commence by holding a meeting to determine its name, constitution, and conditions of membership; but an irrepressible spiritual power took possession of men's souls, drew them together in brotherly love, and made its influence felt in the course of human history, before the necessity for these expedients was discovered. In the absence, then, of any authoritative declaration, we can only gather from the general tenor of the writings which have been preserved to us, and from the nature of the controversies which are there referred to, the uniting principle of the first Christians, and the speciality in their belief which, through the world's sectarianism rather than their own, forced them into an attitude of separation.

Opening now the New Testament, not to discover formal definitions or dry statements of dogma, but to ascertain the source of that wonderful spiritual enthusiasm, that outburst of religious light, which from its obscure home in Palestine soon traversed the vast extent of the Roman empire, we have not long to seek. Instantly there rises into view one great Person, whose name perpetually recurs, and is mentioned with profoundest reverence and love, whose influence pervades every thought and glows in every feeling, and whose faith, seizing with holy contagion upon the heart, gives a triumphant peace to the martyr. We are quickly satisfied that we are reading the writings of men who have experienced a great spiritual change, all the noblest elements of whose nature have been stirred to their depths, and who are conscious that they have entered upon a higher form of character and risen to the apprehension of truer principles; and when we inquire into the source of this change, we are invariably referred, under God, to Jesus Christ as the Being whose teaching enlightened, whose example directed, and whose love constrained them. Now if any one will reflect upon this constant reference to Christ, and consider the way in which his Spirit is held up as the finished beauty of man's filial character, if he will attempt to measure the impression which Christ left upon the hearts of his disciples, and notice how the earliest Christian thought clusters around his person, he will have no difficulty in concluding, without regard to particular passages, that some sort of faith in Christ, combined with heartfelt love and gratitude towards him, was the distinguishing mark of the first believers.

This general impression, derived from the whole structure of the New Testament Scriptures, is perhaps more instructive than anything we can glean from particular statements torn from their connection. The seeming indifference of the writers to mere forms of speculative belief, united with their ardent affection for Christ, and their intense faith that his Spirit was the one true Spirit for themselves and for all men, might suggest much serious reflection and self-questioning to Christians of later times. This impression, however, is fully confirmed by the

examination of single passages. So far as we are
able to ascertain any fixed condition of membership
in the early Church, it was contained in the simple
profession of belief in Christ; and when we look
for some formula to express this belief, we find none
more definite than the following:—That Jesus is
the Christ, or Lord; that God sent him; that he
is the Son of God. According to the narrative in
Matthew's Gospel, Peter's declaration, 'Thou art
the Christ, the Son of the living God,' seemed to
Jesus himself all-sufficient, and to betoken on the
part of Peter a rare spiritual insight and superiority
to mere conventional opinions:—' Flesh and blood
hath not revealed it to thee, but my Father who is
in heaven.' In the writings ascribed to John the
very highest moral and religious power is attached
to this faith:—' He that believeth on the Son hath
everlasting life;' ' He that cometh to me shall never
hunger, and he that believeth on me shall never
thirst;' ' He that believeth in me, though he were
dead, yet shall he live; and whosoever liveth and
believeth in me, shall never die;' ' The Father
himself loveth you, because ye have loved me, and
have believed that I came out from God;' ' Whosoever shall confess that Jesus is the Son of God,
God dwelleth in him, and he in God;' ' Whosoever
believeth that Jesus is the Christ is born of God.'
These strong words sufficiently indicate that this
faith, whatever was its precise nature, was considered

absolutely sufficient for the demands of the Christian life. It satisfied the hunger of the soul, transfigured death into life, and raised man to the most intimate communion with God. A faith which could accomplish that was a saving faith; and to insist upon any lower belief as essential was to interfere unwarrantably with the freedom and power of the new life.

This negative position is brought out most clearly in the epistles of Paul. Attempts were early made to contract the boundaries of communion, and reduce the Christian Church to the level of a sect. Men were scandalised at the latitudinarian tendencies of the great Apostle. Peter and Apollos, and Paul himself, however unwillingly, had their respective partisans, and there was an active Jewish section perpetually endeavouring to narrow the terms of communion, to make sectarian capital out of the new movement, and bind the law of Moses as an irremovable yoke upon the necks of believers. To Paul these attempts seemed tantamount to a total abandonment of the Christian position. Those who consented to be again entangled with a yoke of bondage, and to have their liberty circumscribed with anything less than the universal spirit of a regenerate humanity, had fallen from that grace in which men were free, bound only to worship, and love, and serve in the spirit of the crucified. Nothing else would he consent to preach,

either to subtile-minded Greek or superstitious Jew ;
no other foundation would he permit to be laid ;
and with prompt decision he brought back every
variance to the test of Christ's spirit of love. To
him Christ appeared, not as the head of a sect, as
some at Corinth seem to have thought him, but as a
Redeemer—one who broke every bond and let the
oppressed go free, one who called men from the
stifling and blinding atmosphere of party into the
pure light and refreshing gales of spiritual worship
and allegiance, and who led all who had the courage
to trust him into direct communion with the Father,
far above the world's turmoil and the fierce conten-
tions and mutual exclusions of ecclesiastics and sectaries. Henceforward all men were to be fully
persuaded in their own minds, and, in simple fealty
to the Spirit manifested in Christ and felt in themselves, to work their own duties and think their own
thoughts.

The words of our text express the view of the
Apostle with remarkable conciseness. Among other
manifestations of narrow views in the Church at
Corinth, there seems to have been a disposition to
attach especial importance to certain gifts of the
Spirit, and particularly to those which were most
transient and least valuable, and to use these as a
test, if not of a man's Christianity, at least of his
admission into its inner life. St. Paul reminds his
friends that the simple abandonment of idolatry,

and acknowledgment of Christ as Lord, was the true proof of the Spirit's power, that the Christian life admitted a vast variety both in thought and practice, and even that its completeness was dependent upon this variety. The one thing which showed that a man was not under the power of the Christian Spirit was to pronounce Jesus accursed; while, on the other hand, no one could confess him, at a time when confession must be sincere, without proving thereby that he belonged to Christ, and owned the power of his Spirit. This brings before us the solemn issue to which these first Christians were committed, and presents in its simplest terms the greatest controversy in which human passion has ever been enlisted, or the Divine aid implored. Was Jesus accursed, as Jewish Synagogue and Roman tribunal affirmed, or was he, as the Christians said, a spiritual Lord, whose words were words of wisdom, and whose example it would be well to follow? Was he a pitiful impostor, who met a fate which he richly deserved, or was he the divinest whose voice had ever thrilled into human hearts, and who fell a victim to the world's sin? Who was right, the priests who found him guilty of blasphemy, and crucified him for the honour of God, or He who, by his patient submission and unfailing love, commended the Divine Spirit to the souls of men? Where was salvation to be found, in worshipping idols by order of the state, in submitting to creeds

and forms by order of a priesthood, or in taking up
the cross and following Him? These were the
questions which agitated men's minds—not the petty
topics of debating societies, nor disputes about vest-
ments, incense, or books, but life and death questions
—on the solution of which the future of our race
depended.   Presented in this way, Christianity, as a
moral judge, probed the hearts of men, and drew a
sharp line of demarcation between two irreconcilable
tendencies.   It enlisted on its own side all who were
able to appreciate moral grandeur stripped of its
conventional dress, all whose hearts were awake to
the holiest instincts of humanity, all who sighed for
that only true freedom which is grounded on the
spiritual perfection of our being.   Opposed to it
were stolid conservatism, blind bigotry, unreasoning
prejudice, moral cowardice, and the despairing rage
of that would-be religious infidelity which, secretly
conscious that the heart is devoid of faith, defends
with shrieks of terror each ancient prop, feeling
that if one be touched, the whole rotten edifice will
crumble in the dust.   Between these opposing views
men were called to decide ; and those who refused
to call Jesus accursed, and, daring to defy the
world's opinion, insisted that, so far from being a
malefactor, he was the Son of God, the most absolutely dutiful, the most divinely loving that ever
breathed, and that his cross, instead of sinking him
to the level of slaves and felons, had raised him to

be ' the Lord of Glory ' among men—those, I say,
who made this confession were accepted as Christians by those who most fully understood what
Christianity was; and it is difficult to imagine on
what pretence it could be urged that these men did
not belong to Christ, in an age when in consequence
of this profession men were cast to the hungry jaw
of the lion, and lighted with their flaming bodies the
streets of Rome. If with us this declaration has
become cold, heartless, and formal—a shrivelled
creed which men may repeat and mean nothing—the
fault is in ourselves. Let us throw ourselves back
into its ancient spirit, and with apostolic courage
and simplicity insist on applying it to every part of
our lives, caring more for the reality than for the
words in which we express it, and we shall find that
faith in Christ is still a transcendent power, opposed
to all worldliness, to all intolerance, to all narrowness of aim and view, sanctifying life with highest
hopes, ennobling it with largest sympathies, and
gilding it with the glory of self-sacrifice. Thus
Christianity, though its name has been often used
for sectarian purposes, brings us back to the universal
test of moral and spiritual excellence; and many
who have been denied the name of Christian, many
who themselves perhaps refuse it, become Christians
in the apostolic sense, for they love and revere
Christ, and have faith in his Spirit, even though
they may not call it by His name; and many, alas!

have forfeited the name, who, in weak imitation of others, have insincerely called him ' Lord, Lord!' but have not kept his commandments, and have had no true appreciation of his pure, loving, courageous and self-denying spirit.

III.

THE CHRISTIAN'S DISTINCTIVE FAITH.—III.

ROMANS i. 3, 4.

'*Concerning his Son Jesus Christ our Lord, which was made of the seed of David according to the flesh; and declared to be the Son of God with power, according to the spirit of holiness, by the resurrection from the dead.*'

IN my last discourse I endeavoured to ascertain the fundamental faith of Christianity, as it appears in the earliest records of the religion. We found that, in the opinion of its wisest teachers, the heartfelt acknowledgment of Jesus as Christ, or Lord, or Son of God, was sufficient to show that a man spake by the Holy Spirit, and that his religious life flowed in its true channel. Without seeking any precise definition of these titles, I attempted in a general way to bring before your minds the nature of the controversy which they excited, and to show that they had far more of a moral, and less of what may be called a technical, signification than they have possessed in later times. Of the three terms, 'Son of God' seems to possess the deepest meaning, and to be

most suggestive of further thought; the other two
are in themselves indefinite, and we have no clear
statement of the meaning which was attached to
them.   The word 'Christ,' or 'Anointed,' denotes
simply one consecrated to an important office, and,
taken in connection with Jewish ideas, one who ful-
filled the national expectation of an ideal servant
of God.   The word 'Lord' denotes properly one
having power or authority, and is commonly applied
to the head of a family.   It is frequently used in the
parables of the master of slaves; and if we may judge
from St. Paul's description of himself and others
as servants or slaves of Christ, we may suppose that
the title of 'Lord' was borrowed from this relationship.   But as St. Paul was not literally a slave, as
he boasts of the freedom which he enjoyed in Christ,
as there is not a trace in his writings of subserviency
of judgment, and as he contends strenuously against
subjection to any merely external authority, we may
perhaps fairly conclude that with him the title
'Lord' was not descriptive of any official power or
position, but expressive of moral reverence; and this
conclusion is confirmed when we see in the Apostle's
life, combined with complete intellectual liberty, a
no less complete moral surrender to Christ's Spirit,
constituting at once his slavery and his freedom.   If
we remember that under the gentle influence of
Christ's love he emerged from the dark night of
bigotry, which had filled his mind with delusions

and his heart with hatred, into a breadth of view, a clearness of faith, and a self-devotion to the good of man, which to this day the world does not understand, we can in some degree appreciate the depth of gratitude, the fulness of affection, with which he spoke of Jesus as his Lord—his Lord, yet not a ruler to bring him into 'bondage again to fear,' but a quickening Spirit to redeem; reigning, not by right of office, but by right of holiness; the most lordly because the most self-sacrificing. Christ's rule, the Apostle thought, was in the heart; if a man had not his Spirit, he was none of his; and our true confession is made, not with our lips, but in the reverent and loving submission of our lives to that same mind which was also in Him.

The expression, 'Son of God,' may require a somewhat more lengthened inquiry. Here, too, we are without the advantage of any precise definition of what the Apostles meant; and we can infer the signification of this title only from the ideas which it naturally suggests, and from the connection in which it is introduced.

The term 'Son of God,' which, be it remembered, is used of others besides Christ, seems to convey three main ideas. It suggests, first, spiritual likeness to God. The perfect Son is 'the express image' of the Father, and reflects his Spirit of truth, love, and holiness. Sonship suggests also an intimate communion with the Father, and the reality of a Divine Word within the soul. A son does not approach his father through agents or symbols, but has a direct access to him; and so there is an audience-chamber where God's children may worship in spirit and in truth, and listen for themselves to the command of duty or the pleading of love. And, lastly, sonship implies dependence, a spirit of humility and trust and submission. Here the likeness between Father and Son passes into contrast. The Father gives, the Son receives. The Father looks down with free and unbought benignity; the Son looks up with an adoration that is due. The worthier the Son, the more profound is this sense of dependence, the more absolute the loving obedience to the Divine command.

Such are the ideas which are naturally contained in the expression, ' Son of God'; and I think it will not be denied that these ideas are presented with remarkable clearness and power in the life of Christ. His lowly submissiveness is at least as distinctive a trait as the loftiness of his claims; and these claims themselves arise from his consciousness of communion with God, from the depth of his conviction that, if only men would listen to them, the oracles of truth within the soul were not dumb, and that the Spirit which he breathed was not an earthly exhalation, to be puffed out of existence like the idle breath of priests and rabbis, but ' the eternal Spirit ' which to as many as received it gave power to become Sons of God. This coincidence between Christ's life and the natural meaning of the title so solemnly given to him may induce us to suppose that the natural meaning is also the true one.

We have now to inquire whether this first impression is confirmed or destroyed by the actual scriptural use of the term.

First, let us notice how St. Paul employs it. The nearest approach to a definition of the words that I am aware of is contained in our text. Christ was sprung from David according to the flesh, but was the Son of God according to the spirit of holiness. This, so far as it extends, exactly corresponds with the meaning which we have already sketched. Christ, in St. Paul's view (and in his own, as we know by his question to the Scribes), was the son of David merely by virtue of his natural descent, but was not his son in spirit—not, as the Jews expected, a second David, a great national hero; by his Spirit of holiness, so far transcending that of David, and placing him at once in the position of a superior, he claimed a higher Sonship, and bore a grander likeness. Thus, in the solemn opening of his greatest epistle, St. Paul is content to exhibit that view of Christ's Sonship which in later times has been thought a mean and dishonouring one, only because men always think meanly of that which is too high and spiritual for their comprehension. The objection which is usually urged against this view

is the very thing that made it so fascinating to
the Apostle. It is that sonship of this kind may be
shared by others. This is thought derogatory to
Christ; and yet St. Paul's loftiest flights of reasoning depend upon this very assumption :—' Because
ye are Sons, God hath sent forth the Spirit of his
Son into your hearts;' 'Whom he foreknew, he also
did predestinate to be conformed to the image of
his Son, that he might be the first-born among many
brethren ;' 'He that raised Christ from the dead
shall quicken your mortal bodies : for as many as
are led by the Spirit of God, these are Sons of God ;
. . . the Spirit itself testifies that we are God's
children, and, if children, then heirs, heirs of God,
and joint-heirs with Christ, if so be that we suffer
with him, that we may be also glorified together.'
In accordance with this reasoning, ' the manifestation of the Sons of God,' seemed to him the end
and aim of creation ; and nothing but the life of
Christ within the heart, nothing but ' the Spirit of
adoption,' crying 'Abba, Father !' transfiguring man
from a mere creature and servant into a Son, and
raising him into that direct personal communion with
God which then, as so often since, brought upon all
who believed in it the hatred of the world and the
persecution of the Church, would satisfy his aspirations for mankind.   Not as depreciating Christ, but
as interpreting through him the Divine ideal of
human nature, he argued from the Sonship of Christ

to that of man; and in that crucified and glorified
One he found his own true relationship, and read the
secret of his destiny; he too should pass through
suffering into glory, through death into life, through
the abnegation of all things into the possession of all
things. Oh! how dark must have seemed the time
of his ignorance, when he was certain that God
spake to Moses, but had never a word even for the
holiest of living men, and when life's highest duty
appeared to be to chain up that Spirit which bloweth
where it listeth, and is no respecter of persons or
denominations; and now, he knew that a greater
than Moses is not far from any one of us, and that
faith as of a child in Him unlocked the doors of
salvation, revealed the righteousness of God, and
broke the fetters of 'the law of sin and death.' Is it
wonderful that he spoke of Him whose finger had
cleared his scale-dimmed eyes as *the* Son, the
greatest, the first-born? Such expressions denote
preeminence, a difference, not in kind, but in degree.
And while I cannot assent to an interpretation,
which, by changing the nature of Christ, and calling
him Son of God in a sense totally different from
that in which the term is applied to others, renders
the Apostle's argument incoherent, and shatters the
noble fabric of doctrine which he has reared upon
the Sonship of Christ, I feel that no language is
too strong to express the Saviour's preeminence, or
in the least exaggerates the sentiment which the

D

contemplation of his life ought to awaken in our hearts.

If we turn now to the writings of St. John, we receive, though in a different phraseology, substantially the same idea. In the Gospel Christ's likeness to God, his communion with him, his dependence on him, are all asserted with remarkable emphasis. These, I think, will be found to constitute the most prominent features in St. John's picture of Christ, if, at least, we add this further fact, that they are ascribed to Him with a fulness to which no other can lay claim, and He is represented as the perfect Son, possessing such glory as a father bestows upon his only-begotten, and as One who was chosen to represent this Sonship to the world, and to be the means of leading men into that only true life, the life of God's children. But here too the distinction is one of preeminence. Before Christ is introduced at all, we are told of men who received the Word, and thus owning the voice of God within them had a higher than mortal birth. We can hardly avoid comparing the declaration, 'as many as received him, to them gave he power to become children of God,' with St. Paul's, 'as many as are led by the Spirit of God, they are Sons of God.' The two sentences appear identical in meaning, and both assert the doctrine of human sonship in its broadest terms. This doctrine, with which the Gospel opens, is not forgotten in its course. All Christ's power and

wisdom are ascribed to the indwelling of the Father,
and Christ's own absolute submission to his Word;
and the same indwelling is promised to the faithful.
'If any man will do his will, he shall know of the
doctrine;' the disciples were to share their Master's
glory; the spirit of truth was to dwell within them;
the Father Himself loved them; and not only would
Christ, when snatched from their mortal sight, dwell
in their grateful memories, and all that he had said
and done become clear to their purer inward sense,
but the Father would come and make his abode with
them.

In the First Epistle of John the same thoughts are
set forth in a different form. 'The eternal life' was
manifested in Christ in order that all might share
that life. The disciples' fellowship was to be not
only with one another, but with the Father and with
his Son Jesus Christ. With the Father they would
have the fellowship of spiritual likeness and devout
communion, walking in the light as He is in the
light, being anointed by Him and knowing all
things, approaching Him in confession and prayer.
With the Son they would have the further fellowship of lowly dependence and submission, keeping
the commandments of God, and laying down their
lives for their brothers. That the epistle speaks of
Christ as the Son of God in a sense which is at
least ideally applicable to others may appear from
the identity of the language in which the relation-

ship is described in the two cases. 'God dwelleth in him, and he in God,'—an expression which describes generally any child of God,—is as strong as any language which is applied to Christ in the Gospel, and is exactly parallel to the words, ' I am in the Father, and the Father in me.' That this is a deliberate thought is evident from the way in which it is reiterated, and from the wonder and thankfulness with which the writer contemplates the reality of man's sonship,—' Behold what manner of love the Father hath bestowed upon us, that we should be called children of God.' The words may have been old; but their meaning was new; for Christ had shown what it was to be a Son, and every child of God should be baptised with the same spirit of holiness and the same fire of purification. John felt with Paul that no love could be too deep towards Him whose influence had penetrated to the centre of his heart, radically altered his spiritual position, and changed him from a child of earth to a child of God; and no greater blessing did he think he could confer upon mankind than in spreading around him the same regenerating power which had wrought so mightily in himself, that others might share in the same fellowship, and their joy, like his own, might be full.

Thus the meaning which the expression ' Son of God ' naturally conveys to our minds is confirmed by an examination of the most doctrinal portions of the New Testament, and I know of nothing in the remaining portions to alter our conclusion. In a brief discourse much is necessarily omitted which might seem worthy of examination ; but my aim is rather to sketch out a few suggestive thoughts than to enter into details which would be more suitable to a lecture-room. I wish, if possible, to make these ideas *live* before the mind, leaving it largely to your-selves to verify or reject.

And now, before we conclude, let us glance at the agreement between this fundamental demand of Christian faith and the broad, practical nature of the controversy which, as I endeavoured to exhibit in my last discourse, the first believers maintained against the world. The doctrine that Jesus is the Son of God, as it has been here interpreted, stands out as a living spiritual truth in contrast to a mere metaphy-sical speculation, and at once commands our highest moral and religious sympathies. Opposed to this doctrine were, not intellectual difficulties which might fairly leave it open to doubt, but worldliness of thought, the stagnation of traditional conceptions, and that spiritual deadness which led so many to scoff at the idea of man being anything higher than an intelligent, pleasure-seeking, dying brute. Those who were conscious of a higher relationship, who were weary of a superstitious and unbelieving world, and sighed to escape from dead works and ordinances into the presence of the living God, gladly welcomed

it, and saw in Christ the fulfilment of their vague
aspirations, and the pledge of a redeemed humanity.
Those who accepted the doctrine in this sense had
indeed the witness in themselves; and still that
blessed witness abides with us, testifying to our
spirits that we are children of God, and assuring us
that the true, the beloved Son is known by his
righteousness, his love, his self-surrender to the
higher Will. Thus the difference between those who
believed and those who denied that Jesus was the
Son of God passes from the region of dogma into
that of spiritual character. Their faces were set in
opposite directions, earthward and heavenward. The
one party tended more and more towards the darkness and isolation and bondage of estrangement from
God, and sank into deadening reliance upon formali-
ties; the other expatiated in the light and freedom
of Sons, and felt the stirrings of an immortal power
through their trust in the living Father. To those
whose sympathies are narrow, and whose self-im-
portance is large, it may seem a poor thing that the
fundamental faith of Christianity should be a belief
which many who follow not with them can hold with
profoundest sincerity. But those who have really
felt the touch of Christ's spirit will recognise the
grandeur of a truth which is held by universal
Christendom, and beyond the recognised limits of
Christendom admitted, with the rarest exceptions, by
every wise and noble-hearted man. The great, the

good, the holy are united in a loving reverence for Him who more brightly than any other reflected the Divine image, rose into the nearest communion with God, and committed himself with the most perfect trust and dependence to his Father's will. They clasp brotherly hands across the limits of a merely sectarian Christianity, bound to one another by the fellowship of their common aspiration to have the same mind which was in Him, and knowing that 'as many as are led by the Spirit of God, they are the Sons of God.'

IV.

THE GREAT PURPOSE OF CHRISTIANITY.

JOHN xx. 31.

'*These are written, that ye might believe that Jesus is the Christ, the Son of God; and that believing ye might have life through his name.*'

IN the preceding discourses I endeavoured to ascertain, and to bring clearly before your minds, the fundamental faith of Christianity. We saw that in its earliest form it was simply an undefined faith in Jesus Christ. When it began to seek an intellectual expression, and to assume the more precise language of a doctrine, it was at first content with the statement that Jesus is the Son of God. We found reason to believe that this title was used in the sense which it naturally conveys, and denoted Christ's spiritual likeness to God, his communion with him, and his dependence on him; and that when Jesus is spoken of as *the* Son, the article is intended to imply, not difference of kind, but preeminence of degree.

From this fundamental position, various inferences

may be drawn, and formed into a Christian theology; and these inferences, according as they are well or ill drawn, will constitute a worthy or a mean embodiment of Christian truth.   The superstructure is reared by human skill, and therefore liable to perish; and those who have learned to distinguish the Divine basis from the faltering efforts of man's ingenuity will not be dismayed by the constant transitions of thought, and the crumbling away of ancient systems.   It would have been well for the interests of charity if the Christian Church had clearly recognised this distinction, and profited by the counsel of the Apostle Paul, who warns us that we ought to judge men, not by the superstructure, which they may build of the most various materials, but by their constancy to the one foundation which all occupy in common, and that many will be saved, although the systems of philosophy, or the contrivances of party zeal, which they have so laboriously raised, may be consumed in the fiery trial of human progress, and the paltry materials of which they are composed become evident in the daylight of larger knowledge and deeper wisdom.   But this very liability of our systems to perish, while it ought to make us more charitable and less dogmatic, ought also to render us more cautious and prayerful in their construction; and it is with no overweening confidence, as though all wisdom resided with us, but in the humble hope that the thoughts which I endeavour to present may for a time serve as vehicles to convey living truth to our souls, that I ask for your attention while in this and some future sermons I attempt to exhibit a few of those truths which appear to me to lie nearest the foundation, and to result immediately from the position which we have already gained.

One of the most important questions with which we can occupy our minds, one intimately connected, not only with our whole scheme of theology, but with the direction of our practical life, is this,— what is the great purpose which Christianity is intended to fulfil? The answer to this question may, I think, be stated in general terms thus:—the object of Christianity is to bring a higher and truer life to mankind; and, if we wish to express briefly the nature of this life, we may say that it is the life of children of God.

This view appears to follow naturally and safely from our fundamental position. If the distinctive feature of Christianity consist in the acceptance of Jesus as the Son of God, then the purpose which it will be best adapted to fulfil must be to bring the spirit of sonship to our hearts. Only those who are capable of receiving this spirit can have faith in a Son of God, for they alone can understand him; and the immediate tendency of such a faith is to quicken and develope in us all that is filial. To receive of his mind, to participate in his life, is the direct consequence of faith in him, and may indeed be taken as the measure of that faith. We may have various thoughts and opinions about him which bear no fruit in our lives; but faith in him must gradually transform us into his image. Thus Christianity is an agency for developing the ideal life of humanity, and helping forward that great consummation towards which the world is struggling with groans and travail, 'the manifestation of the Sons of God.'

It is interesting to observe that this view, which follows by way of inference from our primary conception of the distinctive principle of Christianity, is clearly recognised and enforced in the Christian Scriptures. It thus becomes evident that it is no strange or far-fetched or later inference from some heretical mode of regarding Christ's religion, but was enfolded in the original idea of the Gospel, and was considered a matter of superlative importance by the Apostles themselves. The view of Christianity as a principle of life occurs so frequently in the New Testament that I need only remind you of a few of the expressions which are there found. Near the close of St. John's Gospel we have the two doctrines above referred to placed in juxtaposition, and apparently implying the very inference which we have ourselves adopted;—'These are written, that ye might believe that Jesus is the Christ, the Son of God, and that believing ye might have life through his name.' In the same Gospel Jesus is spoken of

as 'the bread of life;' as having come that men 'might
have life, and that they might have it more abundantly;' as speaking words which are 'spirit and
life.' So St. Paul speaks of 'the law of the spirit of
life in Christ Jesus,' making him 'free from the law
of sin and death;' of the 'life and peace' resulting
from 'the spiritual mind;' of 'bearing about in the
body the dying of the Lord Jesus, that the life also
of Jesus might be made manifest' in his body; and
of Christ himself as a 'quickening' or life-giving
'spirit.' Of precisely the same import is the comparison of Christ to a vine, of which the disciples
are branches; for the branches share the life of the
parent stem. Of similar meaning are such expressions as, 'put ye on the Lord Jesus Christ;' 'that
Christ may be formed in you;' 'it is no longer I that
live, but Christ that liveth in me.' There are also
passages which represent it as a main object of
Christianity to turn men from sin to righteousness,
or from dead forms to a living worship; and we must
add those places to which I have referred on a
previous occasion, in which men are described as
Sons of God, and perfect sonship is represented as
the end of the Christian life. This view of Christ's
religion as a life, the life of the Son of God within
the heart, is a pervading thought in the New Testament, and some of its most interesting portions are
unintelligible till we have clearly apprehended this
grand idea.

And now, in order to enter more fully into this idea, we must draw a very important distinction, which is sometimes lost sight of, between the inner and the outer life. We have frequently heard the statement that 'Christianity is not a dogma, but a life;' and properly understood, this formula very well expresses our modern aspirations in their struggle against the oppressive systems of the past. But it may be understood in a very shallow sense, as implying that religious truth is a matter of small importance, and that all which religion requires of us is a certain rough conformity of our actions to a not very exact moral code. That we may guard ourselves against a view which would rob life of some of its noblest elements, let us endeavour to fix in our minds the following distinction.

We may regard life, in the first instance, purely in its outward aspect. In this view life consists of a series of actions, which we may observe, and classify according to the effects which they produce. We may say that some are useful, others injurious; some pleasant, others disagreeable. But if we consistently confine ourselves to the outward view, we can say nothing of the motives from which they spring, or the character which they indicate; for these lie within, and cannot be brought under the notice of the senses. No one has ever seen or heard intelligence, affection, or holiness. If there are such things, they belong to an inner world, which is revealed, not to our senses, but to our consciousness. Strictly speaking, therefore, all that we immediately *know* of our fellow-men is that they do certain things; but whether they do them as machines or as persons, from selfishness or from love, we can judge only by an inference which steps beyond the world of sense, and enters a sphere as invisible as the abodes of the blessed. However clear this may be to our thought, it is impossible for us in practice rigidly to observe the distinction between the outward and the inward; for by an inevitable law of our nature we are constantly making the passage from what we see to what we believe, from the outward and transitory sign to the inward and abiding reality. But although it is impossible for us completely to detach our view of conduct from inferences in regard to character, still we may fix our attention predominantly upon the outward deeds of men, and shift the motives, as it were, into an obscure back-ground. We may content ourselves with regulating public action, and, if only we secure the desired end, care little for the source from which the work issues. This regulation of conduct is the aim of law. Men can enforce certain actions; but they cannot enforce dispositions or affections, partly because our feelings are not immediately dependent on the will, partly because their existence does not admit of absolute proof, and it is unjust to punish men for anything that does not rest upon certain evidence. Accordingly, the law-giver directs his attention, not to the inner, but to the outer sphere of life. He draws up rules to regulate the conduct, and, if the rules be observed, troubles himself no further. We must have contracts kept, violence repressed, decency maintained, whether men are bad or good; and if the commandments be not broken, the legislator has nothing to do with depravity of heart or baseness of desire. Now we are all in danger of carrying this legal view beyond its proper limits, and becoming content, in ourselves and others, with a mere outward conformity to con-ventional rules. We may learn to value life, not for what it intrinsically *is*, but solely for what it *does*. We may so exalt activity above thought and feeling as to forget that its real worth depends upon the thought and feeling behind. And in religion we may extol a feverish energy of work at the ex-pense of devotion, and disparage lonely communion with God, with its resulting depth of sentiment and delicacy of feeling, in comparison with the shallow restlessness of a sectarian agitator. If this be the frame of mind which we denote when we say that Christianity is not a dogma, but a life, if we mean by that assertion that Christianity is nothing more than an outward conformity of our actions to a certain law, we commit an egregious mistake. We are in this case but substituting one outward thing for another outward thing, both of which may be

alike dead. Action and dogma are equally the expression of a life within, and may be equally precious
so long as they are flooded with that life. But from
both the life may depart, leaving them the hollow
relics of a spirit that once breathed, but breathes no
more.

To understand, then, the view that the great
purpose of Christianity is to communicate life, we
must look deeper than the outward appearance, and
turn from the public field of observation to the quiet
retreats of consciousness. We must no longer
consider merely the utility of actions, but have
regard to their motives, and remember that our life
consists primarily, not in what we *do*, but in what
we *are*. Actions are but the manifestations of inner
forces; the forces themselves constitute the essential
life. As a difficulty is sometimes felt in detaching
this idea of inward life from the course of conduct
to which our attention is generally directed, we may
perhaps gain a clearer view by comparing man with
some lower animal; for instance, an ape. The ape,
as far as bodily organisation is concerned, could
probably do the same things as a man, and he can
actually counterfeit many human actions. But if
we attempt to penetrate into the inner life, how
vast the difference! The ape cannot solve a mathematical problem, nor breathe in verse the sorrows of
his soul, nor discuss the advantages of political
measures, because his intelligence is of so low a

type. So, again, he cannot pass sentence upon sin, or kindle with the glow of faith, or kneel in worship, because conscience and the spirit are either absent or asleep. We see that the ape's deficiency is in the inner forces which constitute the glory of a man. In the same way the great differences among men themselves are to be found within. One man has a larger intelligence, or a deeper insight, or broader sympathies, or a keener conscience, or a more devout heart, or more tender affections, or greater energy of will than others ; and it is within, among those unseen forces, that the battle of life is to be fought by each. Legislate as we may, a life of grand and noble actions can never be generated from mean and unconsecrated powers. The most that law can do is to repress. To create is beyond its power ; and even in repression it has always met with a very partial success. The volcano of passion must have its vent ; and however stern the law, society will have its tremors of struggling vice and falsehood. If we would regenerate men, we must begin within ; if we would communicate life, we must give enlarged spiritual power. And when we say that the aim of Christianity is to bring a higher and truer life to mankind, we mean that it aims at cleansing the inner fountains of our thought and feeling, imparting a new heart and a new soul, developing and quickening our best faculties, exalting our affections and desires, and making us

keenly alive to the solemn relations in which we
stand, and the holy significance of our being. And
when we say that this life is the life of Sons of God,
we mean that Christianity aims at bringing men into
the spiritual likeness of God, raising them through
the consecration of the heart to perpetual communion
with him, and making them humbly conscious of dependence on his fatherly love. Thus the Christian
life is neither a dogma nor an action, but a certain tone
of thought and sentiment, a certain purity of desire
and simplicity of aim, a certain holiness of affection,
spirituality of devoutness, humility of self-dedication.
From this inner life will issue both doctrine, the
expression of Christian thought and sentiment, and
action, the expression of Christian desire and will.
But these may change, though the life remains
essentially the same. As the spirit gains in depth
and power, and man becomes more truly a son. the
sentiment may struggle for higher standards of
doctrine, and devotion press for new forms of
activity. Doctrine and practice are the changeful
vestures; the communion of the soul with God in
the Spirit of the Son is the abiding essence. And
this is life, the highest that a created being can
share, eternal life because a wavelet from the life of
God.

Brethren, this doctrine at which we have arrived
is a solemn one, giving us a standard of awful purity
by which to test our Christianity, snatching us away

from all deceiving forms, and bringing us face to
face with God in the hidden sanctuary of the heart.
Have we received this life, or is Christianity still to
us a name, having indeed a traditional halo of reverence round it, but devoid of power to redeem us
from sin, and clothe us in the sanctity of Christ?
Do we prize more than all our theories, more than
all our sectarian schemes, more than our worldly
ambitions and success, the crucified self-will, the
Christ formed within, the Spirit of the Son in our
hearts crying, ' Abba, Father?'   ' Hereby shall all
men know that ye are my disciples, if ye have love
one to another;' ' Love one another as I have loved
you;' "If a man have not the Spirit of Christ, he is
none of his;' 'If I have not love, I am nothing.'
This is the serious issue to which our doctrine
brings us; and if we may glory in its simplicity, its
grandeur, and its spiritual power, we may in that
proportion deplore the dulness of our hearts in so
feebly apprehending it, and the poverty of lives so
little hallowed and ennobled by its quickening
breath.   Oh! that it may come with a new meaning to our souls, and enable us henceforward to bear
the fruits of the Spirit, and live as becomes the
children of the Most High.

V.

CHRISTIANS A ROYAL PRIESTHOOD.

REVELATION v. 9, 10.

'*They sung a new song, saying, Thou art worthy to take the book, and to open the seals thereof: for thou wast slain, and hast redeemed us to God by thy blood out of every kindred, and tongue, and people, and nation; and hast made us unto our God kings and priests: and we shall reign on the earth.*'

IN my last discourse I sought an answer to the question, what is the great purpose of Christianity? and we saw that the main object which the religion is calculated to effect, is to bring to men a fuller inward life, the life of children of God. The proper apprehension of this object will enable us to enter more deeply into the genius of Christianity, and give a peculiar direction to our views upon a variety of subjects. Let us consider at present some of its more general bearings.

One of the first things which would powerfully impress us, were it not for a deadening familiarity with words of lofty meaning, and perhaps also the baleful influence of a corrupt theology, is this—the wonderful faith in human capability implied in such an object. When we speak of man as a child of God, we are carried into a sphere of unknown magnificence, whose beauties stretch far beyond our present vision, and whose aspiring heights, overtopping the clouds of earth, rest in the eternal light of heaven. We see now through a glass darkly, and know not yet what we shall be; but all of great, and holy, and wise, and true, which saint can conceive or prophet declare, all this and more is wrapped up in our sonship. Now what an unconquerable faith in human capability must have been that which first seized upon this truth, and determined to lead on our race to such a glorious heritage! How grand the faith which looked beneath the sins, and follies, and superstitions of men, and recognising amid their stupid sleep the God-like powers of the soul, dared to say to each, thou too art a son of God; thou too mayest put off the garment of shame, and be clad in robes of white in thy Father's kingdom. This faith, expressing itself in various forms, is the spring of all truly Christian effort, sending apostles to toil amid the idolatrous vices and degrading luxuries of a heathen empire, and impelling missionaries to travel into strange countries in order to mitigate the fierceness of rude barbarians, or to seek at home the abodes of sin and misery in order to carry the light of higher truths or the softening influence of gentler manners to those who have forgotten their birth-

right. The endeavours of philanthropy, sanitary
and educational improvements, acts of political
justice, reforms in the treatment of criminals, all
owe their zest to this same faith that there are
immeasurable capabilities in the human breast, and
that the future of our race may be greater than its
past. Nor shall this faith cease its loving work till
the brute nature in us is fully tamed, and every
child of man reflects, with unveiled face, the glory
of the Lord.

But this very aspiration, which is always pointing
to the future, reminds us that man is not yet
complete, but, if I may so express it, the Son of
God in us is struggling with elements of meaner
birth. The purpose to which Christianity addresses
itself implies the need of redemption, or deliverance
from some sickly or imperfect state; for we do not
send a physician to those who are in health, or
implore those to act as sons ought to do who
are already discharging every filial duty. Accordingly, when the light of Christ's Spirit is turned
upon our hearts, we become conscious, not only of
divine possibilities in ourselves, but at the same time
of present disorder and imperfection. The sense of
sin is proportioned to the clearness with which we
have discovered the hidden man of the heart; and
those in whose ideal human life flashes back, as a
pure mirror, the Divine image, rises into hourly
communion with God, and subsists in conscious

dependence on his love, must often sigh at the darkness which clouds their souls, and send up many a prayer for deliverance from their frailties and sins. The highest view of our relation to God is the most conducive to humility; and the revelation is simultaneous of our true goal, our distance from that goal, and our inadequacy to reach it without our Father's help. It may be remarked in passing that on these contrasted and mutually revealing facts in our nature, our sonship and our sin, must depend the doctrines of Christian redemption and of divine grace; but for the present another aspect of the subject demands our attention.

Whatever may be the precise means of redemption, the two facts above mentioned, the possibility of sonship, the actuality of sin, are universal facts; that is, they are not the characteristics of any special nation or any single period. God has made of one blood, of one nature, all nations of men; and if we are called to depart from sin, and live as becomes children, it is simply by virtue of our human birth. It is for this reason that Christianity aspires to be a universal religion. It appeals to man as man; and, disregarding the specialities of race, seeks to develope that spiritual life which, whether bearing already the fruits of righteousness or folded in the yet unopened germ, belongs to every soul. It was the full perception of this truth which delivered St. Paul from the exclusiveness of Jewish pretensions. The Jew, condemned by his own law, stood as much in need of redemption as the Gentile; the Gentile, however lost in sin, had a nature as intrinsically God-like as the Jew. Both were children of God, because both were men; in each the consciousness of sonship slumbered; in each it might be wakened to vivid life: and both had access by one spirit to the Father. Therefore it was that worship passed from its centre at Jerusalem, and, ceasing to depend on local and temporary ceremonies, consecrated the whole earth, claiming living hearts for its temple, and offering up ' spiritual sacrifices ' to Him who is not far from any one of us.

The reasoning which in the mind of St. Paul placed Jew and Gentile upon the same level, does away also with the distinction between priest and layman. Communion with God is not limited to any sacred order, nor do we require any ghostly benediction pronounced upon our offerings of love and duty, in order to render them acceptable. The prayer in spirit and in truth breathed in the secret chamber is dearer to God than the most imposing ceremonial performed in obedience to ecclesiastical authority. The highest spiritual privileges are open to us as men. God is nearer to our souls, and hears our confessions with a deeper sympathy, and enjoins a holier penance, than any priest. The veil hangs no longer before the holy of holies: and the space between the cherubim has filled the universe with its sanctity. The sacerdotal order has opened its ranks ; its nearness to God is a distinction no more ; every man may approach, and, with the spirit of consecration resting upon him, present his own prayers and his own 'spiritual sacrifices.' Christ has redeemed us 'out of every kindred, and tongue, and people, and nation, and has made us unto our God kings and priests.'

It appears, then, (and the question is not unimportant at the present day, in connection with the High Church movement,) that in resisting the claims of every form of sacerdotal religion, and disowning the special sanctity and authority of a priesthood, we are not denying any doctrine which expresses a larger faith than our own, but in obedience to faith are withstanding what seems to us the denial of a great Christian truth. The assumption of authority is a denial of the supremacy of conscience. The claim to be the only legitimate administrators of religion is a denial of the nearness of the soul to God, and of the filial relation in which every man stands to the universal Father. The pretence that certain forms of worship are necessary to salvation, and that these forms depend for their efficacy upon a select order of men, is a denial of the supreme value and saving power of worship in spirit and in truth. However slight may be the probability of England ever returning under the

dominion of priests, yet at a time when men influential both by intellect and character are working in
this direction, it is well that we should see plainly
the religious ground of our opposition to all ecclesiastical assumptions, and learn to prize more than
we do the privileges of our freedom. In the middle
ages, distinguished, as they were, by that credulity
which results from want of faith, sacerdotal religion
was permitted to bear its full fruits ; and one of its
saddest features was that deep-seated infidelity to
which it owed its power. This will perhaps become
evident in an interesting way, if I read from the
glowing pages of Dean Milman his account of a
papal interdict which rested upon England early in
the thirteenth century :—

'Throughout England, without exception, without
any privilege to church or monastery, ceased the
divine offices of the Church. . . . The churches
were closed, the bells silent; the only clergy who
were seen stealing silently about were those who
were to baptize new-born infants with a hasty
ceremony : those who were to hear the confession of
the dying, and to administer to them, and to them
alone, the holy Eucharist. The dead (no doubt the
most cruel affliction) were cast out of the towns,
buried like dogs in some unconsecrated place . . .
without prayer, without the tolling bell, without
funeral rite. Those only can judge the effect of this
fearful malediction who consider how completely the

whole life of all orders was affected by the ritual
and daily ordinances of the Church. Every important act was done under the counsel of the priest
or the monk. Even to the less serious, the festivals
of the Church were the only holidays, the processions
of the Church the only spectacles, the ceremonies
of the Church the only amusements. To those of
deeper religion, to those, the far greater number, of
abject superstition, what was it to have the child
thus almost furtively baptized; marriage unblessed,
or hardly blessed; the obsequies denied; to hear
neither prayer nor chant; to suppose that the world
was surrendered to the unrestrained power of the
devil and his evil spirits, with no saint to intercede,
no sacrifice to avert the wrath of God; when no
single image was exposed to view, not a cross unveiled : the intercourse between man and God utterly
broken off; souls left to perish, or but reluctantly
permitted absolution in the instant of death?'*

Such is the religion of a priesthood! God is at a
distance from his creatures, and meets them only
through the intervention of a priest; normally
absent, only exceptionally present. The sacred
order is silent, and God's love is thereby banished
from the world, and the guilty soul trembles under
that wrath which only the mighty spell of an ec-
clesiastic can avert. How all this vanishes like a
dark dream before the truth that Christ has made us

* 'Latin Christianity,' vol. iv. p. 11.

unto our God kings and priests! The churches may
be closed, but the blue vault of heaven is not
canopied in black.   Oracles may be mute : but the
still, small voice in our conscience is not muffled.
Officials may curse; but the Father breathes his
blessing in the trustful heart.   Councils may forge
their ghostly fetters ; but the sons of God are free,
and 'we shall reign on the earth.'

The difference between these two conceptions of
religion may become more strikingly apparent, if I
read you a few lines by Dr. Newman descriptive of
the Mass, and placing that rite in its most attractive
form.   The description occurs in a supposed conver-
sation between a Catholic and a Protestant :—

'The idea of worship,' Willis replied, 'is different in the Catholic Church from the idea of it in
your Church, for in truth the *religions* are different.
Don't deceive yourself, my dear Bateman,' he said,
tenderly; ' it is not that ours is your religion carried
a little farther,—a little too far, as you would say.
No: they differ in kind, not in degree; ours is one
religion, yours another. . . . I declare, to me,' he
said, and he clasped his hands on his knees, and
looked forward as if soliloquising, ' to me nothing is
so consoling, so piercing, so thrilling, so overcoming
as the Mass, said as it is among us.   I could attend
Masses for ever, and not be tired.   It is not a mere
form of words,—it is a great action, the greatest
action that can be on earth. It is, not the invocation

merely, but, if I dare use the word, the evocation of the Eternal. He becomes present on the altar in flesh and blood, before whom angels bow and devils tremble. This is that awful event which is the end, and is the interpretation, of every part of the solemnity. Words are necessary, but as means, not as ends; they are not mere addresses to the throne of grace, they are instruments of what is far higher, of consecration, of sacrifice. . . . They are the words of the Lord descending in the cloud, and proclaiming the Name of the Lord as He passes by, "the Lord, the Lord God, merciful and gracious, long-suffering, and abundant in goodness and truth." And as Moses on the mountain, so we, too, "make haste and bow our heads to the earth, and worship." So we, all around, each in his place, look out for the great Advent, "waiting for the moving of the water."*

There is much in this passage to captivate the imagination; we cannot but admire its fervent strain of piety; and it is well that we should know that this form of religion still possesses the vitality and the power of faith. But when we attempt to analyse the emotion which is described, it appears to arise from a combination of scepticism and love of the marvellous. That God should appear in flesh and blood upon the altar excites more rapturous devotion, and seems a more real presence, than the

* 'Loss and Gain,' pp. 290-292.

breathings of his Spirit in the heart, the solemn warnings of conscience, or the self-sacrificing deeds of men who, under his leading, have consecrated themselves to their Father's service. And what a deep unbelief is contained in that word, which even the writer hesitates to use, but which yet is the key to the whole priestly conception of religion, '*evocation* of the Eternal'! Have we to evoke, to call from some dim recess, or summon from a distant throne, Him who dwells within the contrite heart, Him who has searched us and known us, and to whom in the almost oppressive consciousness of his nearness we raise the cry, ' whither shall we go from Thy Spirit, or whither shall we flee from Thy presence?' The adoration which bows the head before the uplifted host need not wait upon the forms of the Church; for nowhere can we turn our thoughts, within or without, and not find enough to fill us with reverence, admiration, and love. Oh! it is our cold, dull hearts that need to be evoked, and not that blessed Father in whom ' we live, and move, and have our being,' and who by a thousand and ten thousand mercies seeks to win our worship and devotion. Sacerdotal and spiritual religion are indeed ' different religions.' The one would summon God from His clouds and darkness; the other, believing that God is light, would scatter the darkness of the soul. The one would appease the avenging wrath of the Almighty, and bring him tranquillised to his children; the other, believing that God is Love, would tame man's rebellious will, and bring it in meek submission to a Father's feet. The one sees God most clearly in the exceptional, the strange, the terrible; the other finds him most in the divine order of creation, in blessings daily given, and in that still centre of our being where his calm voice rebukes our passions and our fears. The one invites us to a fitful and mediatorial communion; the other would fold us for ever in the bosom of our Father, and consecrate the whole of life with the spirit of worship and love.

But, it may be asked, if all men are thus invited to share whatever is spiritually grand in the priestly office, what is the use of ministers of religion, and what is the sphere of Christ's own work? I reply, that the value of the Christian ministry depends entirely on its power of reaching and elevating the soul of man. It has no magic key by which to open the kingdom of heaven. It has no form of evocation by which to summon the Great Spirit from his obscurity. It can offer no prayer which will be accepted as a substitute for yours. It can do nothing *for* you, except so far as it works *in* you. It may remind you of great truths which you are in danger of forgetting, or appeal to holy sentiments which are beginning to slumber, or give form and expression to your feelings of contrition, of aspiration, or of faith. But every duty towards God belongs to you

as much as to the minister. You must love Him as
deeply, adore Him as reverently, serve Him as faithfully. You too are sons, with a duty to discharge,
a divine race to run, a God to glorify; for 'in
Christ Jesus we are all the children of God by
faith.' Our highest hope as ministers is to be
helpers of your joy, and to be the lowliest servants
in that 'royal priesthood' to which we all belong.
And for Christ himself the highest glory is that he
touches the heart with heavenly power, regenerates
the soul, and kindles the consciousness of sonship.
We must receive him into our hearts, if we would
derive any benefit from him. His work on our
behalf must be within. He came to impart his
own filial spirit, that we too, quickened with the
breath of a higher life, might enter the holy of
holies. It was for this he died; and, grateful for
the precious gift, we will take up our song, 'Thou
art worthy; . . . for thou wast slain, and hast redeemed us to God by thy blood out of every kindred, and tongue, and people, and nation, and hast
made us unto our God kings and priests; and we
shall reign on the earth.'

VI

CHRIST A QUICKENING SPIRIT.

1 CORINTHIANS xv. 45.

' The last Adam was made a quickening spirit.'

IN my last sermon I endeavoured to show that, in the Christian view, whatever is spiritually noble in the priestly office is open to all men, and that those who have been consecrated by the Spirit of Christ, whatever may be their calling in life, constitute a ' royal priesthood.' We saw that in relation to this view the exclusive pretensions of every sacerdotal religion present the appearance, not of the assertion, but of the denial of a truth, not so much opening a pathway of communion as closing all but one special approach to God, and claiming as the private property of a caste what belongs to mankind. At the conclusion we touched upon one or two thoughts which require a fuller treatment; and this we may now attempt in answer to the questions,—on what natural wants does the belief in the priestly office rest, and how are those wants satisfied by Christ?

F

That priesthoods are not the mere offspring of imposture, but answer to some deep and general want in our nature, will be readily admitted by every calm student of history and of the human soul. There are certain feelings within us, aspirations, and hopes, and fears, which every form of religion seeks to satisfy; and the rudest response to these feelings is better and truer than a cold disregard which virtually denies their reality, or with cynical contempt derides them as unworthy of notice. In opposition to an unspiritual and mammon-worshipping civilisation sacerdotal religion is an advance, though in reference to Christ's religion of the Spirit it is a retrogression; for it at least recognises and meets, however imperfectly, our permanent religious wants, and in the midst of worldliness bears witness to a divine Majesty above the world, whose rights must be admitted, and whose judgment is to be feared. To understand this more fully we may notice one or two of our most conspicuous needs.

There is, first, the sense of sin. Whatever precise form this may assume, whether the superstitious fear of having given some personal offence to the awful Power above us by the neglect of prescribed ceremonies, or the purer consciousness of having violated a law which is the expression of divine righteousness, and of everlasting obligation, there is the same feeling of alienation, of coldness, of distance between the soul and God. There is the attendant sense of responsibility, with its apprehensions of a judgment to come, or the shame and contrition which result from the present judgment of the conscience. These feelings, however they may vary in different individuals, belong to our common nature, and cannot be exorcised either by the sneers of the flippant at hearts more sensitively strung than their own, or by the sophistries of a shallow and unspiritual philosophy. The gay Felix trembles at the secret thought that every wrong must be redressed; and the saint, with clearer conscience, sees the precise shadow that lies between himself and God. The idolater shudders at calamity as an outburst of avenging wrath; and the Christian, with a holy ideal ever in his heart, mingles an undertone of sadness with his most rapturous praise. Under this consciousness of sin we turn to religion, and the value of any form of religion depends in part upon the answer which it can return to the cry of a conscience oppressed with the burden of guilt, and seeking for peace and light amid its own darkness and confusion.

There is another sense of want, which, if not so universal, yet arises in certain stages of the religious life. It is a sense, not of sin as a positive and wilful violation of the divine law, but of frailty and blindness, of weariness and perplexity. We are often conscious of a wavering faith and of flagging affections, far unlike the piercing vision and untiring

fervour of love which we think we ought to have.
How little do we realise the great truths of religion!
With what feeble force do we carry them into the
practical concerns of our lives! How perpetually
are we lapsing into formalism, and offering to God
only half our hearts! How difficult is it sometimes
to see the light of a Father's love shining through
the cloud, and to feel, while we say, that he is
good! How hard to be always gentle, patient, and
submissive, and to offer that sacrifice, which yet is
ever at hand, the sacrifice of our own wills! Here
are wants which cry aloud for rest. Our souls
thirst for God, for the living God; and yet how
often, seeing him no more, can we only remember
him as from a strange land! Oh! to return, and
behold him, as we have seen him in the sanctuary;
but the way seems long, and the night dark, and our
feet are weary. 'Oh! that we were as in months
past, when the secret of God was upon our tabernacle, when the Almighty was yet with us;' but
how strange and hollow sound these voices from the
days that are gone! and, dry and callous, we feel no
sacred and mysterious presence in our abodes.

From these reflections it may appear that there
are deeply-rooted wants in our nature to which
every form of religion must address itself; and it is
not surprising that any form which can, in however
imperfect a manner, satisfy these wants should
obtain a certain amount of support. Famished men

are ready to fill themselves with chaff, and superstition, lavish in its promises, is ever at hand for
those who are weak in faith. Now how does sacerdotal religion respond to these sorrows and aspirations of the soul? By consecrating a special order,
to stand, as it were, midway between the common
heart and God, to act as the only authorised inter-
preters of his will, the administrators of his justice,
and the instruments of his grace. This, I think,
fairly represents the position of the Roman Catholic
priesthood; and that it is no exaggeration of High
Church pretensions may appear from the following
quotations from an Anglican publication :—'Our
Divine Lord appointed a ministry in His Church,
whose office it is to administer the means of grace to
its members ; . . . consequently, no one can take this
office on himself without a direct commission from
CHRIST. . . . He appointed His disciples, in the first
place, to be Apostles, with a power to transmit their
commission to others, as the needs of the Body
required. . . . Without this commission no acts are
valid, and no ordinances have any assurance of grace
attached to them.'* 'The Protestant bodies in
Europe form no part of the one Body, because they
have renounced the one Priesthood. . . . They have
cut themselves off from participation of the one
Spirit.'† It is easy to understand how, in conformity

* 'The Church and the World,' First Series, p. 184.
† Ibid. p. 187.

with this view, our spiritual wants will be dealt
with. Oppressed with the consciousness of guilt,
we must betake ourselves to the priest, who is not
merely a brother man who through his superior
wisdom or piety may help us by his advice, but
the representative of God, who speaks with Divine
authority, and issues his commands in the name of
that awful Power against whom we have offended.
To him we must make our confession; he enjoins
the needed penance, and pronounces that judicial
absolution which alone can restore our peace. We
come away with the blessed sense of pardon, and
the wound in our conscience is healed. So too, if
we long to be nearer God, to hear his voice more
clearly, and to love him with a purer devotion, the
intercourse which we desire may be maintained
through the medium of a priest. He can present
the sacrificial offering which God will receive from
the hands of the ordained. He will utter miraculous
words of consecration when our own prayers seem
winged with lead; and he will perform those mysterious ' ordinances ' which bring us into ' participation of the one Spirit.' Thus we escape from a god-
less world, and in the bosom of the Church behold,
if not God himself, at least the veils behind which
he dwells, and we witness those rites through which
he communicates himself to the souls of believers.
We depart with awe, perhaps too with our faith and
love renewed; for we have been on holy ground, and

have looked upon God's own vicars in the discharge of their most sacred office, and have wondered at the condescension which stoops from heaven to speak to us through these chosen ones, the priests of the most high God.

From this sketch we may perceive that sacerdotal religion gives a very real answer to our religious wants, and, seen from the world below, may well appear majestic and imposing. Regarded from any point but the highest spiritual religion, I can easily imagine that it may seem even to refined hearts and powerful understandings all that is attractive, consoling, and elevating ; and the reasonings which are urged against it are often rude attacks upon its abuses rather than calm objections to the principle itself.

But although the power of a priesthood, if exercised according to its ideal (which it never has been), might be most salutary in restraining irreligion and worldliness, it must not be forgotten that by its fundamental principle it must restrain other things of incomparably higher value, and it fails to satisfy the profoundest wants of our souls. If it checks the free license of sin, it no less bridles the rights of conscience, and assails with coercive tyranny every movement of intellect and soul which does not complacently glide in the groove which it has cut. In other words, it denies the Divine authority for each man of his own conscience, and of what, in the humble exercise of the powers which God has given him, he believes to be true. It is utterly unable to comprehend that in rejecting its authority men may be acting, not from self-willed license, but in deference to a far higher and nearer authority, and that the Spirit of God within the heart may speak with a clearness and power which admit of no appeal. For this submission to the authority revealed within, which has ever characterised the grandest minds, priesthoods have nothing but sneers and crucifixion ; and they condemn as blasphemy what is in truth obedience to God rather than man, and therefore the highest act of reverent self-sacrifice. And in regard to the satisfaction which priestly religion offers to our spiritual wants, it fails, I think, to reach the depths. Under the consciousness of sin, we need something more than the assurance of forgiveness conveyed through a messenger ; we would feel God's own love in communion with our souls, and gain a holier life in the fulness of his presence. In lonely, silent prayer we would own the touch of his Spirit, and escape from the weary burden of our selfishness into the sweet rest of hallowed affections and filial service. We would lay for ourselves, upon an altar not made with hands, our very sin as a sacrifice to be consumed away, and, with a trust too sacred to be breathed in human ears, hide ourselves in Him whose salvation is never far from the broken and contrite heart. And when with less distinct con-

sciousness of guilt we mourn our darkness and coldness, how poor the comfort to be told that we may
hear the sound as God passes by, or even gaze
upon his flesh and blood, which, even if we admit
the extreme doctrine, can never be more than
material symbols of Himself! Why must he pass
by instead of making his abode with us? To what
purpose the mystery on the altar, if the heart be
still empty of his presence? To look with earthly
eyes on any symbol of him, however marvellous,
is not to know him. We might gaze for ever, and
yet not have heard his voice at any time, or seen
his form. This hearing must be inward and spiritual,
and unless the light of God's Spirit flash directly on
the consciousness, we may be told of it, but cannot
know it. Thus sacerdotal religion, though it may
speak with true authority to the worldling, and
constrain him to believe that God is nearer and more
awful than he thought, yet says in effect to the
Christian that God is colder and more distant than
he had fondly believed, and is not the Father who,
in spite of sins and doubts and perplexities, has
seemed so long to tabernacle in his heart. For the
one it is an advance towards spiritual truth, but
even for him an advance which must end in the
suppression of the very faculties to which spiritual
truth appeals; for the Christian it is simply a
relapse towards denial and unbelief.

And yet it is true that we need help in following

the religious life, and that under the consciousness
of sin and in our thirst for God we turn instinctively
to nobler spirits than our own, and seek their aid
and guidance. It is here that Christ, whose influence
with more or less fulness is perpetuated in Christian
institutions, comes to our relief. He is a mediator,
not in the sense of interposing between us and God,
but as showing us the Father, and leading us too
into the sanctuary where we may worship and listen
for ourselves. He is 'a quickening Spirit,' revealing in his own life the way to the Father, which we
are so constantly tempted to forget, and, by impress-
ing on truth and righteousness the glowing colours
of reality. giving them an absorbing and vivifying
interest. Under the consciousness of sin he changes
our selfish dread into a sad sense of the long-
suffering love which we have wounded; by his
tender sympathy he consoles us; and when in utter
self-distrust and anguish of heart we cry, 'Make us
as thy hired servants,' he lifts our bowed heads to
see a Father's smile of welcome resting on us. He
brings us to God, and, having filled our souls with
the peace of renewed faith and love, leaves us in this
blessed communion. Further, he helps us to break
the yoke of sin, and does not mock us with hopes of
an illusory pardon while the gift of life itself is denied.
He breathes into us his own Spirit, and while with
the frank uncovered face of sons of God we gather
round him, we are changed into the same image from

glory to glory. It is difficult to construct any
theory which will express the influence of spirit on
spirit; but of the reality of such influence we all
are conscious. There are men whose look, or voice,
or action by some mysterious power enters our souls
and breaks up the ice-bound fountains of our better
life. And who can spend an hour in calmly medi-
tating upon Christ's teaching, or in endeavouring to
penetrate the meaning of his life, or in affectionate
memory of his love and of his cross, and not be a
humbler, a wiser, and a stronger man? Oh! when
dead theories cease to be thrust between us and
Christ, and he is allowed with his own benign power
to enter our hearts, and to tell us what he has heard
with the Father, what we too may hear, and how he
has solved life's problem by seeking that Father's
will, we shall find that he is for ourselves ' a quickening spirit,' and gives us fellowship, not only with
himself, but with God.

Thus Christ is not a mere external authority,
which may curb and lop, but can never vivify; his is
a life-giving power, and his authority is found in the
reverence and love which he awakens in the heart.
He is not merely an instructor whose precepts we
may coldly study, nor an example whose achievements we may stiffly imitate, but, like every creative
soul, he fills us with his own fire, flashes into us his
own moral enthusiasm, and, mightiest power of all,
he captivates us by his love. A pedant in art may

furnish us with rules, and enable us on the principles
of authority and restraint to produce a correctly
drawn but lifeless picture; the man of genius will
communicate what is infinitely more precious than
rules, *himself*, reveal to us the very soul of art,
awaken our dormant apprehensions of the beautiful,
bathe us in the light of an ideal world, and thus
change us from copyists into artists.   So, in the
higher sphere of the religious life, Christ's ' follow
me ' thrills into the soul, calling the dead conscience
from its grave, breathing all around the spirit of
devotion and self-surrender, and thus converting us
from servants into sons.   Hence the Christian is
free; free, not by the rejection of all authority, but
by submission to the highest authority; free, because
he is no longer under tutors and governors, but has
received into his heart the Spirit of the Son; free,
because he is no more in bondage to worldly passions
or superstitious fears, but listens with glad obedience
to the voice of God within his soul, that voice made
audible by Christ, who has unstopped our deaf ears.

Oh! it is strange that this 'quickening Spirit,' this
beloved Son who is in the bosom of the Father,
should be left sadly waiting to flood the world with
life, and make it, what but for man's sin it already
is, a paradise of beauty and gladness.   The up-
holders of authority, each desiring to rule rather
than to serve, wrangle for the supremacy in a divided
Christendom, and allow the gentle Saviour, who

seeks not to coerce but to quicken, to mourn in the outer coldness. His plaintive reproach still sounds, ' Ye will not come to me, that ye might have life.' But yet his own shall come from east and west and north and south, and with him bow in worship, listen to the word of God which dwells within, and take up the duties of a filial service. And these, though never called by a common name or included in the muster-roll of a common Church, shall have a blessed unity, not the unity of prisoners bound to one another by the iron chain of oppression, but the unity of brothers who, quickened by the same Spirit, are the conscious Sons of the one universal Father.

VII.

THE NATURE OF REVELATION.

JOHN xiv. 9.

'*He that hath seen me hath seen the Father.*'

1 CORINTHIANS ii. 10.

'*God hath revealed them unto us by his Spirit: for the Spirit searcheth all things, yea, the deep things of God.*'

THE former of these texts suggests to us three connected subjects of thought—the nature, the means, and the object of revelation. If we rightly apprehend these subjects, we shall see that they are not merely topics to exercise the ingenuity of theologians, but involve questions of profoundest interest for every one of us. Theology has fallen into disrepute on account of its idle wranglings and its vexatious interference with advancing knowledge; but it needs only to be restored to its true relation to our practical life, and to address itself to the problems which weigh with a secret burden of anxiety upon the mind of the age, in order to enlist once more the serious attention of all earnest and cultivated men. Questions about the authorship of books, or the precise accuracy of certain ancient records, though they have been discussed with so much noise, are but surface problems, about which men pursuing exactly the same methods and holding the same principles may legitimately differ. They do not touch the heart of any great subject, and men might solve them either way, and yet remain in the densest ignorance of God. But the question whether we can know God at all, whether he is indeed our Father, in living communion with every soul, or, at best, the unknown and unknowable author of certain laws, is one that reaches the very heart of religion, and the solution of which must affect the entire complexion of our lives. It is a question which, if we have risen at all above the animal, must press upon us with more or less eagerness of claim. Are we surrounded by impenetrable mystery, observant only of successive changes, but knowing nothing of the eternal ground that underlies these changes? Are we conscious of dependence, but dependent on we know not whom? Are we haunted by a sense of responsibility, but utterly ignorant of the spirit of our judge? Do we mourn our imperfection, and yet know nothing more perfect than ourselves? Or is there a revelation of God, and, if so, what is the nature of that revelation?

In bringing before you some very imperfect thoughts upon this difficult subject, I know not that

I can more briefly or clearly state the view which I wish to illustrate than by saying that revelation consists essentially, not in the imparting of information from without, but in the opening of the spiritual eye within. It has been common to speak of revelation as though it were a miraculous statement of facts or truths, of the reality of which we could not be otherwise assured; and the trustworthiness of these statements has been supposed to rest upon evidence originally addressed to the senses, and made known to us by the testimony of competent witnesses. The Bible, it is said, embodies this miraculous statement, and in order to understand revealed religion, you have simply to examine its meaning, as you would the directions of a legal document. Now it would be unwise to attack this view as radically false; for, as it has given satisfaction to a large number of minds, it probably contains an element of truth, and it may be taken to represent, though, as I think, in a rough and inaccurate way, the outward element of revelation. But it seems to me utterly insufficient; and the most exquisitely drawn and divinely authenticated statement cannot, I am persuaded, constitute a revelation till—

'The Spirit breathes upon the word,
And brings the truth to sight.'

The inadequacy of this view may appear from the following considerations.

It is practically unable to create religious faith.
It may be doubted whether a mind sceptical in
regard to religion has been ever brought to recognise
the reality of God or of immortality by the mere
study of evidences. Entangle the sceptic as you
may in the web of your logic, convince him triumphantly of the unreasonableness of his doubt, and
still the icy spot remains upon his soul, waiting to be
thawed by the fire of the Spirit. Or supposing that the
mind has never questioned the evidences of religion,
but is perfectly satisfied that the form of doctrine in
which it has always been intrenched is impregnable,
is there therefore religious faith, or may not God be
superseded by the dogma, and the creed be worshipped while the Divine admonition is blasphemed?
It is not by the presence or absence of articulate
doubt that the degree of faith is to be measured,
but we must apply a more practical test. If a man
assured you that a wall was on the point of falling,
and then, although if it fell it would bury his mangled
body in its ruins, he went and sat composedly under
it, you would feel confident that he was trifling
with you, and did not really believe what he said.
And are we to presume, however loud may be their
protestations of faith, that when men are coarse, or
selfish, or irreverent, or distrustful, they have any
deep conviction that eternal Holiness and Love and
Wisdom surround them as an atmosphere, and pierce
to the very centre of their hearts? Surely in such

G

cases the religious creed, though it may be honestly
accepted as a true theory of spiritual things, is yet
nothing more than a form of the understanding,
and has never attained to the dignity and power
of faith.   From these instances we may conclude
that, while in scientific matters reasoning upon the
testimony of our senses is able to give us complete
practical convictions, in the sphere of religion something more is required.   Our reason may ascertain
the philosophic ground of our faith, express it in
logical form, and determine its relations with science
and with life, but cannot generate it.   As in physical
science the intellect can only work upon the facts
which are furnished by the senses, and our scientific
faith ultimately resolves itself into trust in the vera-
city of our senses, which we are content to accept but
cannot prove, so in religion the office of the reason is
to work upon what it receives from our power of
apprehending the deep things of God, and religious
faith is due to a faculty in the soul which is turned
towards God, as our senses are turned towards the
earth.   If our apprehension of what is Divine has
never been awakened, or, being awakened, has lost
its delicacy or allowed its force to be destroyed, we
can have no living faith ; and in order to receive
the refreshing gift, we need, not a greater logical
subtlety, but a greater capacity of soul.   We may
thus understand what, I think, is so often observed,
that where there is the greatest dogmatism there is

the least faith; for dogmatism is satisfied with the logical completeness of a theory, and rests on the process and the form rather than on the reality which it undertakes to describe; but faith arises from opening the eye of the soul, and while it gazes directly on its object, discovers how unfathomably deep are the things of God.

Again, the view that revelation is simply an authoritative statement of facts or truths is insufficient, because such a statement, however perfect, could not communicate the deepest knowledge. There are limits beyond which it cannot pass. It may tell us something of what God has done, of what he intends to do, of what he requires us to do; but Himself, his Spirit, his character, the communion between us and him, it cannot reveal. Words, in order to be intelligible, must represent thoughts or ideas in the mind; and unless their meaning be first revealed within, it is in vain that they are used. A document relating to spiritual conditions which you had never experienced, referring to feelings or emotions with which your heart had never thrilled, or describing the nearness of a love to which there was no response within, would be no revelation; it would either convey no meaning whatever to your mind, or induce you to form very erroneous conceptions of the subjects which it brought before you. The real nature of sin and of righteousness, of repentance and forgiveness, of

justice, mercy, and holiness, must be revealed in
our own inward experience, or they cannot be
known at all. It is in vain that you reiterate that
' God is love,' if my terrified conscience and cruel
temper shut out the very notion of love, and empty
the word of all true meaning. The Spirit of love
must dawn upon our consciousness; no mere description will enable us to understand it; but as
soon as its light arises within, a revelation is made,
and the spiritual mind apprehends what was hidden
from intellect and sense. Thus it is that the wise
and prudent may be grossly ignorant of that which
is clear as day to many an unlettered heart. The
most powerful intellect can only proceed upon the
data which are furnished to it; and if the deep
things of God have never passed across the field of
consciousness, it may speculate in vain as to their
nature or requirements. A single glance of spiritual discernment would often necessitate the demo-
lition of the most elaborately constructed schemes
of theology; and as long as our spirit is of the
world, we may move round and round the temple of
truth, but cannot enter its inner shrine. This is
doubtless one reason why the New Testament has
received such varying, and, as I cannot but think,
such inadequate interpretations: the key to unlock
its mysteries must be found in our own hearts, and,
if I may so express it, only the Christ within us
can understand the Christ of history. It is for this

reason, too, that St. Paul, referring to his own experience, says that God revealed his Son, not to
him, but in him. He had known Christ after the
flesh; he was aware that he had said and done
certain things, and had been crucified; and the
crucifixion he had regarded as a triumphant refuta-
tion of his claims, and as covering him with well-
merited contempt. But when the Spirit of the Son
flashed into his heart, and enabled him to understand for the first time the lowly submission, the
complete self-abnegation, the all-surrendering love,
and the communion with God a thousand-fold more
intimate than could be obtained through law or
ceremony, which characterised the true child of God,
he instantly perceived that the Man of Sorrows, who
himself bore our griefs and carried our infirmities,
and was made sin for us that we might be made
the righteousness of God, was indeed the divinest
among men, the hope, not only of Israel, but of the
world. His change came, not from fresh evidence
addressed to the reason, but from raising of his
spiritual level; and what eye, and ear, and intellect
had sought in vain, God had revealed by his Spirit.
The veil was taken from his heart; and in the light
of a higher authority he recognised for the first
time what was most divine in those very Scriptures
which he had always misread while he believed
their authority to be ultimate. Resting on the
nearer authority of the Spirit, he beheld Law and

Psalm and Prophet glowing with a new meaning ; and while he forsook the tables of stone, he found the Divine Will written on the tables of the heart. So must it be with us. 'The letter killeth; the Spirit giveth life.' So long as we regard the Bible as a mere external authority, intended to give us a knowledge of religion without our having the trouble of being spiritual, it will bring no holy message, no true revelation to our minds. The truths which are spiritually discerned we cannot know till the Spirit which searches the deep things of God comes and makes its tabernacle in our souls.

The above view may be made clearer by a simple illustration. Let us suppose that a man has been imprisoned all his life in a dark chamber. The beautiful world is all around his dungeon walls, but he neither sees its loveliness nor hears its harmonious sounds. To him it is a mystery, solemn, vast, impenetrable. Now, how could the world be revealed to such a man? Would it be sufficient to send in a messenger to instruct him? The messenger might be gifted with most wonderful powers of description, and yet all his eloquence would be wasted upon that forlorn man. If we can suppose a creature thus secluded to be capable of understanding language at all, he might listen eagerly to what was said; but it is evident that the ideas which he formed would be utterly fantastic, and as remote from reality as that of the blind man who thought that red colour was like the sound of a trumpet. But if, instead of attempting this futile instruction, you bore a small hole through the enclosure and admit a ray of light, you instantly make a revelation. That dim and tiny ray is yet the very light with which the universe is filled; and the imagination may immediately set itself to work to conceive a light infinitely vaster and more glorious than that feeble glimmer. And if you allow the prisoner to apply his eye to the aperture, and to see the distant hills, and shady trees, and waving corn, he will receive an idea, most imperfect, but yet true as far as it goes, of the appearance of the world. So in spiritual things, our minds, impenetrably dark, may be in the very midst of the eternal light, and yet unable to comprehend it. No description will make it plain. Hearing we may hear and not understand. An aperture must be made through the dark prison walls of our lower life, and a beam of holy light allowed to strike the retina of our spiritual eye; and then, though we may know very little, though the darkness may still seem to enfold the struggling light, yet what we know will be real; if not the very fount of Divine glory, yet a veritable effluence from that fount.

We see, then, that revelation involves a fresh act for every one of us, and, considered in its essence, resides not in any record, but is for each a taking away of the veil from the heart. It is not when we listlessly hear even the most blessed words of Scripture that truth is revealed to us, but when new ideas, new feelings, and new aspirations thrill through the soul, and all that is noblest in us vibrates in answer to that thrill. A record may give us precepts to regulate our conduct, but cannot reveal the eternal moral distinction between right and wrong, and show us that it is intrinsically and for-ever good to submit our wills to the Divine. These can be revealed only by the direct gaze of the conscience; and if the conscience be asleep, we may know the form, but not the power, of righteousness. Similarly those higher attributes, which we describe generally as the Spirit of God—his Holiness, Justice and Love—may be spoken of in words which are bathed in the most sacred memories, and lighted with a halo of traditional reverence; and yet these words may sound the merest commonplace to a sensuous or worldly mind; they become expressive of revelation only when the fire which originally kindled them burns within the soul, and ' the Spirit bears witness with our spirit.' And surely I do not dream when I say that we are often conscious of this witness of the Spirit, that we feel it brooding, as it were, over our spirits, but not yet incorporated with them. Do we not *know* a love, a tenderness, a pity, a forgiveness, an impartiality, which we do not yet possess? And do not these things arise in our consciousness with the impress of Divine authority and beauty, and plead with us that they may enter in and take full possession of our hearts? In our wildest passion we know that they are true; in our most restless storm we feel the rebuking touch of a higher peace. If for us the Divine is anywhere, it is here; and this frame, which encloses such strange depths of guilt and error, is also an awful temple of the Holy Spirit. Let us put on, then, the hallowed garment of humility, present the sacrifice of our own will, and bow our heads in the self-abandonment of prayer; and then we shall receive visions and revelations of the Lord, and hear the voice of the Spirit, which 'searcheth all things, yea, the deep things of God.'

VIII.

THE MEANS OF REVELATION.

JOHN xiv. 9.

' He that hath seen me hath seen the Father.'

IN a recent discourse I directed your attention to
the nature of revelation: and we saw that, so far as
it relates to the character or Spirit of God, it consists essentially, not in the imparting of information
from without, but in the opening of the spiritual
eye within. It might be easily inferred from this
that every revelation of the Divine Spirit must be
made directly to the soul, without any intervention
of outward means. We saw that a veil must be
taken from the heart, and God's holiness, justice, and
love disclose themselves in the consciousness, or all
teaching and description must be thrown away. Is
anything more, then, necessary for us than to sink
into ourselves, and listen in mystic meditation to
the oracles of faith within? The experience of
mankind pronounces in the affirmative. God might,

if it so pleased him, communicate his highest revelations by an instantaneous flash to every soul; but
as a fact, he links together inward and outward experience, and makes events and scenes in the visible
world the occasions of new advances in the unseen
life of the Spirit. Light is worthless for the purposes of vision without the susceptibility of the eye;
but the eye, on its part, is equally unserviceable
without the presence of light; and only the combined
action of force without and sensibility within enables
us to see. Thus the sensibility of the soul must be
touched by what passes in the world around it, or it
might sleep for ever, unconscious of its own existence. Without human intercourse, love would never
tremble into conscious being, or be recognised as the
central glory of the Divine Spirit; without gradations
of higher and lower in character, it may be doubted
whether the idea of One who is highest and best of
all would ever dawn upon the mind. But, on the
other hand, these outward things have meaning only
to the soul which is ready to interpret them; and to
the spiritually dead the very voice of Christ might
prove as uninteresting and uninstructive as Raphael's
Madonna to an ape in search of its food. Both elements must be combined in order to bring us to the
knowledge of spiritual truth; and while we regard
the revelation itself as the flash of recognition which
passes between the soul and God, we may consider
as means of revelation some of those outward

agencies by which God appeals to our hearts, and
gives us 'the light of the knowledge of his glory.'

The agencies which are employed to enlarge our
knowledge of God are too abundant to admit of
complete enumeration. Theologians, in their pursuit
of scientific exactness, are apt to seize upon some one
plan of salvation, and devote to it such an absorbing attention that they either deny the reality of all
others, or at least decry them as miserably insufficient. But God's methods of working are far larger
and more varied than theology is inclined to suppose.
Any one mode of revelation may be insufficient, and
yet contribute a very necessary portion to the grand
result; just as soldiers, individually helpless, may,
when formed into an army, defy the enemy's attack.
To the heart turned towards God almost every
event may bring its revelation, either lighting up
recesses of the spirit before unknown, or reviving
and deepening old impressions. The Church and
the world, faith and doubt, poetry and science, reading and thinking, company and solitude, laughter
and prayer, all play their part in enriching our
spiritual experience, widening our field of view, and
so admitting us to a fuller knowledge of God. We
must bear this in mind while we consider some of
the means of revelation; and while we are grateful
for those which appeal to men in successive ages,
we must not forget that we owe an undefined debt
to the special discipline of our own lives, and to the

scenes and associations amid which we have been placed.

We shall probably not be wrong in dividing the means of revelation into two great classes—nature and man. It has been customary to divide religion into natural and revealed. The distinction, however, I cannot but think more artificial than real. If nature reveal God at all, if it communicate or suggest any real knowledge of him, then the religion which arises on the contemplation of nature is revealed religion. Are we to say that Christ taught revealed religion when he inferred the immortality of man from the words said to have been spoken in the burning bush, but only natural religion when he inferred God's kindness to the sinful from the universality of the sunshine? For my own part, I cannot but think that there was more revelation in the second instance than the first; that in the second the impartial sun really suggested, and so revealed the truth, while in the former case an argument was sought in support of a truth already held. If the light of faith arises in the soul, a revelation is made, whether the light proceed from miracle or from uniform law. But the distinction between nature and man is real; for nature, at most, is the unconscious and mute expression of the Divine thought, whereas man is the living temple of God's Spirit, and capable of uttering in articulate form the Word that dwells within him.

Turning now to nature, we may remark that there are two distinct frames of mind in which we may regard it, which we may briefly describe as the poetic and the scientific. In the poetic mood we rely more upon the general expression of nature, and care comparatively little for detailed facts; in the scientific, we lay the whole stress upon the accurate observation of facts, and care nothing for the moral or æsthetic expression. We may expect, then, that if nature bring any revelation to our souls, it will be when we glow with the spirit of poetry and worship, not when we regard its operations with the coldness of science. We may indeed pursue science from a religious motive, and have our religious feelings excited at every step of our progress; but these are only accompaniments, coruscations of light flashed from the adoring soul around our way, and not essential parts of scientific procedure. We cannot demonstrate the existence of God, as we can of electricity, by a course of experiments, or by our most subtile analysis make palpable his love. An atheist may be as accomplished a student of nature as a theist. In saying this, I intend nothing derogatory to science, but simply endeavour to define its province. It is the business of science to examine the phenomena which are presented to the senses, and to determine their mutual relations and the laws of their succession; and these remain the same whatever account we may give of the original cause which lies behind, or of the moral purpose which is in course of fulfilment. Science cannot resolve either way the question whether there is a perfectly righteous and loving Father in communion with the soul; for such a problem does not lie upon its path, and is not amenable to its methods. From the scientific study of nature, then, noble as is the pursuit and wonderful as are its results, we must expect no direct revelation of God. Science has, indeed, indirectly been of inestimable service to theology in clearing away old errors, and so preparing for larger developments of religious truth; but justice, mercy, purity—in short, all spiritual attributes—must be known from some other source, and the most that physical science can accomplish in this direction is occasionally to prove a conformity between the facts of nature and the highest inspirations in the soul.

The case, however, is altered when we turn to the poetic aspects of nature, and regard it, not as furnishing us with knowledge, but as appealing to our sentiments. The scenes of nature are wonderfully adapted to touch our finest sensibilities, and he is not to be envied who can gaze upon its beauty unmoved by religious awe and veneration. Ages ago, the mountain top, hiding itself from the world behind its cloudy veil, and aspiring in silent mystery toward the heavens, appeared a fitting place for worship, and brought home to the eager heart the

reality of One who is clothed with majesty and
power; and the shady grotto, where evening's softest
hues stole between the leaves, and the rivulet, catch-
ing on its ripples the changeful gleam, murmured by
in gentlest cadence, seemed a meet abode for a spirit
of tenderness and benignity. The towering rock,
casting its shadow along the burning ground, and
affording a cool retreat to the weary traveller, has
reminded the soul of that mighty One in whom it
may shelter itself from the fiery trials of life's
journey; and the deep well, of which generation
after generation had drunk, has recalled to the
thoughts that fountain of living water of which every
thirsty soul might drink. Thus every scene may
reach beyond the eye, and touch the spring of some
holy sentiment, and nature, become the changeful
vesture of the eternal Spirit, act as a symbol through
which he holds communion with our souls. To
those who have eyes to see and ears to hear, Nature
has many things to reveal; but in saying this, we
admit that only a spirit already in sympathy with
the Divine can understand her voice. A revelation
must be made from some other source before we can
pass behind the veil of nature; and if we had not
found Love in the intercourse of human life, we
should never find it by roaming over mountain or
plain. The landscape which entrances does not
love us; the stream which allays our thirst feels no
compassion; the bounteous harvest does not pro-

nounce our sins forgiven. Nature needs an interpreter, and not till after we have known God does
she speak to us of his wisdom, his holiness, and his
mercy.

For the fullest revelation, then, we must turn to
man, where we find, not alone a dumb symbol of
thought and love, but a conscious mind manifesting
itself through a marvellously expressive organism.
In man truthfulness, justice, patience, kindness,
purity may actually dwell, and reveal their nature
through countenance and tone, action and language. No one can associate with men of exalted
character without feeling that he understands these
things better, and has looked into depths more
divine than the spirit of ordinary humanity. Love,
beaming from the human eye, reaches the heart
when Nature has no answer to our yearnings; and
there is light around the cross when earth and sky
are dark.

It may be said, however, that precisely the same
difficulty besets us in our intercourse with man
which we felt in the contemplation of nature; we
must recognise the Divine Spirit in ourselves before
we can understand it in another. The tenderest
pleadings of affection will be unintelligible to us,
if our own hearts have never throbbed with the
sympathies of friendship. The rapt look of devotion will be empty of meaning, unless we our-

H

selves have prayed. The mercy which forgives
will seem but folly, unless some higher principle
than self-love has revealed itself in our conscience.
To a certain extent, this is true. That of which
we are by nature incapable we cannot understand.
If it were impossible for us ever to feel love, it
would always remain an unknown force within the
breasts of others; some of its effects we might perceive, but the affection itself we could not know.
But if, on the other hand, our nature be capable of
any spiritual affection, although that affection may
never have risen into distinct consciousness, we
seem able to understand it when it appears vividly
in human life. When we witness a higher excellence than our own, we discover at once a reality
without us and a capacity within. Probably most
men have found for the first time their own religious
life through experience of its kindling power in
another; and they have recognised as the true expression of their own nature that spiritual beauty
which had never made its home within themselves.
Our human charities may have been tied up within
the narrow circle of family or of class, and yet,
because we are Men, the Son of Man may make us
conscious of universal brotherhood. Our filial spirit
may have been buried in deadly slumber, and yet,
because we are Sons, we may hear the voice of the
Son of God and live. Thus the spirit in other men
may act as a light to touch the susceptibility of our

own, and quicken into consciousness our dormant perception of higher goodness.

One other step remains. Is the goodness which is thus revealed the Divine goodness? Yes, for goodness everywhere must be essentially the same, and God is not less, but more, good than his children. That which is highest, purest, most venerable in man is not more resplendent than the Divine character, but only a dim reflection of its brightness. From Him come the love and holiness which adorn the saint; from Him comes also the conviction that these are more divine than hatred and profanity. We never can confound the Holy and the Satanic spirit within us; and as we climb the ascent of goodness we *know* that we are drawing nearer to God. It seems to me that this conviction is written indelibly upon the human soul. No man who feels the impulse of both love and hatred can for a moment doubt which is the more God-like. Therefore it is that, seeking for a higher goodness, we pray for the Spirit of God, and feel that in winning goodness we are gaining, not the transient life of a mere animal, not a mocking shadow and counterfeit of the Divine reality, but the eternal life itself which abides for ever in the bosom of the Father. Therefore it is, too, that in regard to goodness, we can never stop with admiration of the man in whom it is manifested, but lift our praise to God; and while we shout our ready applause at the achievements of self-will, we

bend with awe before that goodness which dwells in
a consecrated heart, and glorify the Father in the
Son.

And now we are prepared to understand our
text.   If in any Son of man the presence of the
Divine Spirit were so full, and the submission of
the human will so devout, that in him were combined the most transcendent loftiness of soul and
the gentlest and most winning love, and all that is
merely of the earth and the flesh lost its hold on the
spirit of his life, and his desires, aims, and affections were caught up into unison with the Supreme
Will, he would be the revealer of God, and in
seeing him we should see the Father.   This is
precisely what Christians have always felt to be the
case with Christ; and when they declare that in Him
they have seen farther into the divine than in any
other, they only utter the experience of their own
hearts; and probably none who have seen him in
the sense which he intended, who have entered by
sympathy into his soul, and apprehended the inmost
spirit of his life, will hesitate to place him at the
head of the hierarchy of saints, and with reverent
gratitude accept him as the beloved Son, 'the first-
born among many brethren.'   Through him God
has revealed his love to many a thirsty soul fainting
with sin and grief; and while his teaching has
sunk into our hearts, the conviction has come that
in listening to him we are listening to the Father

who sent him, that a Divine Word shines amid human darkness, and in him that Word was wholly uncorrupted by the perversities of self-will. Thus we are led to know God, not in the theologian's sense of holding correct doctrines about him, but as a man knows one whom he loves, one with whose heart his own beats in sympathy. The Spirit, which else were silent, or would speak a language that we could not understand, or appeal to hearts too gross to care, wins its way through the fascination of human life; and pleading from a cross, attracts, subdues, quickens the erring and reluctant soul, and fills it with the light of Heaven. But let us never forget that Christ himself cannot give us this revelation by mere instruction. To see him spiritually is to see the Father; but we may see him—as Philip, as the world, saw him—with earthly eyes, and not know him. We may even in our blindness use him to hide from us the deep things of God, and attend him with our ambitious hosannas while he goes to glorify his Father. If we would receive his revelation, we must abide in him and let his Word abide in us, and learn what it is to deny ourselves, and take up our cross and follow him.

IX.

THE REVELATION OF THE FATHER IN THE SON.

JOHN xiv. 9.

' He that hath seen me hath seen the Father.'

IN my last discourse I tried to show that a revelation of God may be made in and through man, and that this revelation is quite distinct in character from that which is made through the material world. Such a revelation, I conceive, is made with more or less clearness in all ages; but it is generally admitted that there has been One among the sons of men in whom it has come with surpassing fulness, and whom therefore we justly accept as *the* revealer of God. The claim thus arrived at on behalf of Christ, that in seeing him we see the Father, suggests one or two lines of thought which we had not time to follow out last Sunday. To these I would now ask your attention.

That such a revelation as we have lately considered, the revelation of the Divine Spirit or character, should be made in Christ, appears to follow directly from what we accepted as the distinctive doctrine of Christianity, namely, that Jesus is the Son of God. Sonship consisting in spiritual likeness to God, communion with him, and dependence on him, it is clear that the Divine nature is manifested in the Son as it can never be in the physical creation, which, though dependent on God, neither resembles him, nor can hold conscious communion with him.

This view may be brought out more distinctly if we consider it in connection with that twofold conception of Christ which has always prevailed in the Christian Church. Looking around upon the theological world, we cannot fail to be struck by the two opposite points of view from which Christ seems to be regarded. On the one hand is the conviction, which has most widely prevailed, that in Christ there is a superhuman element, that in him God has really drawn near to man, and entered within the darkness of mortal life, in order to irradiate it with his own truth and love. According to this conception, we do not see in Christ the spirit of man rising up in search of God, but God coming down to seek and bless mankind. So predominant have been the feelings of awe, and wonder, and devout gratitude at this manifestation of the Divine, that Christ has been regarded as the Omnipotent God himself, in mysterious union with our frail humanity. And by many Christians the human

element seems to be almost forgotten; and while
they bow in veneration before his grace and
truth, they are unable to feel any brotherly relation
with him, and worship him simply as the manifested
God.   On the other hand is the conviction that he
was truly a man, and that in him human nature
ascended towards the Divine, and attained its native
dignity.   He was a great teacher and thinker, but
one who increased in wisdom as well as in stature.
He was a great religious reformer, and discerned by
the light of intuition where the essentials of religion
lay.   He was a martyr, but not a sacrifice, and displayed the endurance of a faithful man, not the long-
suffering of the pardoning God.   He set a grand
example, at which our hearts bound with a respon-
sive throb; and he thereby exhibited the glory of
human nature rather than the benignity of the
Divine.   So complete may be the sympathy with
him, so absorbing and delightful the feeling of
brotherly union, that the Divine element may be
lost from view, and Jesus appear exclusively as the
wise and noble man.   And with many this humani-
tarianism so completely shuts out the other point of
view that the Scripture language which implies
anything more mysterious is rejected as an unwar-
rantable importation from Greek philosophy, the
simple wisdom of the fourth Gospel descends into the
speculative subtlety of the Schools, and the life of
Jesus is read off in the light of ordinary human

history and of the ordinary conceptions of human nature, and pruned of those seeming extravagancies which are so easily referred to the ignorant credulity of his biographers.

Between views so divergent, and in their extreme form so contradictory, it might appear hopeless to find any reconciliation. Yet as each has been held by earnest men as an article of religious faith, and upon grounds which they supposed to be sufficient, it is difficult to believe that either can be absolutely false. May they not be one-sided expressions of truth, resulting from two different tendencies of thought, which are equally legitimate, but must act in combination in order to lead us to a sound result? The deepest minds have acknowledged the necessity of recognising both elements, the Divine and the human, in order to frame a true doctrine of Christ. In the creeds which have been most widely accepted in Christendom, although the Divine element, which at the time when the creeds were drawn up was the point in dispute, receives for that reason the largest share of attention, yet the human has not to complain of any doubtful recognition. In fact, the problem of the Church has been to explain how it is that this magnificent expression of Divine wisdom and love has appeared in combination with human infirmity and suffering. The problem still remains, although we may reject any particular mode of explanation. The so-called Athanasian Creed may be wrong; but the fact is still there. Even if we have recourse to the credulity of mankind, still we must give some worthy account of so grand a delusion, and not dismiss with a silly sneer the heartfelt faith of men gifted with the highest powers of thought and the deepest spiritual insight. Believing—I trust, with all reverence for the thoughts of others—that the ordinary Trinitarian explanation creates more difficulties than it relieves, I venture to think that the doctrine of Christ's Sonship, as we have here understood it, taken in connection with our view of revelation, furnishes the key by which this mystery may be unlocked.

In the first place, if Jesus be the Son of God, we can at once understand that in seeing Him we see the Divine character, so far at least as it is open to human apprehension at all. The qualities which we most revere in Christ, and which leave upon us the most solemn impression—namely, his perfect purity, his impartial justice, his noble truthfulness, his immeasurable love—are precisely those qualities which we instinctively characterise as Divine and eternal. They bear their own witness to the conscience, and refuse to be confounded with the transient displays of human passion, ambition, greed, or sensuality. Wherever we meet them, they command our honour; within ourselves they speak with an authority which we may disobey, but whose rightfulness we cannot dispute. In other

men, the impression these qualities produce upon us
is obscured by a large admixture of lower elements ;
and they appear rather as transient flashes from a
nobler spirit concealed within than as the unclouded
central light which illumines the whole character with
its glory.   But in Christ they constitute, as it were,
the substance of his being, not waging a fierce and
doubtful war with lower impulses, but calmly triumphant, enthroned upon his heart with the serene
majesty of conscious power, and leaving on most
men's minds an impression of unapproachable sub
limity.   It is for this reason that words, which
coming from any one would enforce respect, when
spoken by him seem to be nothing less than the
utterance of a Divine voice.   As though the
righteousness of Heaven had taken up its tabernacle
in human form, the conscience is pierced, hypocrisy
abashed, penitence subdued into tears of devout
love, by the fervour or the tenderness of his appeal.
When He pronounces sin forgiven, it is as though
the Father whispered peace; when He yearns to
save, it is as though the gentleness of God were
bending over our stricken souls.   We feel that in
Him God has indeed come to seek us, and caused
his pity and love to shine amid the shadows of
mortality and sin.   And is not this feeling true?
For what are the love, the justice, the holiness of
Christ?   They surely do not originate in human
selfishness, nor are they invented by human reason

or fabricated by human will, but are simply the indwelling of a Spirit given from above, a Spirit which
reason and conscience may accept, but whose nature
they cannot alter, and whose force they cannot
create.   They are not the dark, ephemeral fancies
of a disordered brain, but the one abiding light
amid the fitful glare of human thought and passion.
They are not the passing wisdom of a single age,
but the eternal Word, which, however dimly discerned, shines as a central light in every man, but
appears in its fulness in Christ, that we too may
receive of its fulness.   Derived, not from earth, but
from God, the immediate offspring of His creative
power, disowning all lower dependence, and constituting the highest attributes which we can ascribe to
God, are we wrong in saying that they are indeed
the Divine Spirit, and that it was the in-dwelling
Father who manifested himself through words of
truth and deeds of mercy?   Thus is justified the
belief of Christendom that in Christ there is a superhuman presence, and in the death on the cross a
more than earthly love was revealed to man.   This
reasoning will indeed apply in a less degree to others
besides Christ; and I believe it true that in every
man there is more than man, and in each bosom a
mystery too deep to fathom—a position admitted by
the Christian doctrine of the Holy Spirit; but vulgar
prejudice dishonours that which is common; and
while in us the human is apt to set up for itself and

obscure the Divine, in Christ it becomes the submissive organ of the higher Spirit, and the glory of the man is made subservient to the manifestation of God.

It will be observed that this view, while recognising to the fullest extent the reality of the Divine Spirit in Christ, yet by no means identifies him with God, and does not claim for him either omnipotence or omniscience. We should expect, indeed, that wisdom, that spiritual insight, and that earnest faith which are associated with the highest forms of character, but we are not obliged to look for dogmatic infallibility, or accept as final every word which is ascribed to him on the most incidental topics. God may have chosen him as the organ of his own righteousness and love, and yet the forms of his thought may have been partly moulded by the ideas of his age. He may possibly have accepted the current and erroneous notions about demons, while it is no less true that the Divine forgiveness breathed through him. He may, perhaps, have been mistaken about his second coming, while yet in him God was reconciling the world unto Himself. Knowledge and power are measured, not by their purity, but by their amount, and can be infinite only in an infinite Being; the Spirit is measured, not by its amount, but by its purity, and may shine with unsullied splendour within the limits of a finite nature.

We are now prepared to turn to the other side of

Christ's Sonship. We shall not be surprised to find this more than royal majesty combined with frailty and limitation. We shall not be perplexed at the weary sleep in the wave-tossed boat, or the fragile form tottering beneath the heavy cross. We shall not regard his worship as an insoluble mystery, nor shall we have to account for the seeming agony of the immortal King. In all this we recognise the man, and feel no inconsistency in the recognition. The love of God may burn its way into the world's history through the words and deeds of a man, and yet leave the human personality untouched. The Son not only inherits the Father's Spirit, but is dependent on him for all things, and, if clothed in human form, must receive the Spirit within the limiting conditions of a mortal and dependent nature. Worship must be the very breath of his life. Without prayer as a link of communion, he would cease to feel the inspiration of the only Good; without the consciousness of frailty and need, he could not discover the filial tie that binds him to the infinite Creator; and in casting off his dependence, and exalting himself, he would abdicate the glory of a Son. So far from dependence and worship involving an apparent contradiction in this view, as they do in some others, they are essential to that very manifestation of the Divine which leads us to believe that, in listening to Christ, we hear more than an earthly voice. Worship, involving a complete surrender of

the human will to the Divine, was the one condition
without which such a manifestation would have been
impossible; and he spake with the authority of God,
precisely because his submission was so absolute,
and he spake not from self, but from that which he
felt to be higher than self.

It is in this feature of his Sonship that we feel our
human sympathies so nearly touched. Here we
recognise the Man, conscious of infirmity, subject to
weariness, hunger, and pain, not ignorant of temptation, keenly alive to the affections of friendship, sad
at the thought of his lonely death, needing the comfort
and support of prayer; yet here, too, in seeing him
we see the Father, and this lowly dependence is as
necessary to a perfect revelation as the clear shining
of the higher Spirit. For the word 'Father' is not a
proper name, but a relative term, denoting one who
stands in a fatherly relation to us. Now a fatherly
relation on one side implies a filial relation on the
other, and cannot be fully manifested without the
presence of a son. We might know God as the
infinitely wise and good, and yet not know him as
the Father. But the beloved Son, who is in his
bosom, has declared him. He has completed the
true relation between parent and child; and in seeing his reverent, confiding love, and patient submission, we see also that blessed One on whom his
heart was stayed, and whose will he followed with
such simple and unchangeable devotion. Thus,

whether we regard Christ as the impersonation of Divine righteousness and love, whose remonstrance breaks the death-slumber of our conscience, and whose appeal kindles our hearts into a sacrifice of grateful affection; or, on the other hand, view him as the Man of Sorrows, whose soul was obedient unto death, and breathed the prayer, 'Not my will, but thine be done'—we still find him the revealer of God, and in seeing him we see the Father.

Time does not permit us to enter into a justification of the above view by examining the facts of Christ's history, but we may briefly observe that there are evident traces of a twofold consciousness in him, answering to the twofold conception which I have attempted to explain. On the one hand, was the consciousness of that within which was higher than self. We see this in his profound conviction that the great principles which he uttered were no idle fancies of his own, but the dictates of unerring wisdom; in his confidence that his judgments were not mere ebullitions of prejudice, but the verdicts of eternal justice; and in the manner in which he called the disciples' attention to himself as manifesting more than an earthly nature. On the other hand, his sense of dependence is no less marked. This not only appears in the worship to which we have already referred, but is expressly asserted: ' I live by the Father,' ' My judgment is just, because I seek not mine own will, but the will of Him that sent me;' 'The words which ye hear are not mine;' 'I can of mine own self do nothing.' We have in him, accordingly, a union of loftiness and humility, of conscious preëminence and unaffected simplicity, of world-wide claims and meekest self-abnegation, which has often proved perplexing, but which, I think, becomes intelligible when we remember that the Spirit of holiness, wisdom and love, which in him has commanded the world's veneration, is from God, and the most that man can do is, with lowly dependence and submission, to receive that Spirit and work out its behests; and that to glorify the Heavenly Father is at once the grandest and the most self-renouncing labour in which it is possible to engage.

Thus it has pleased God to reveal himself through his beloved Son. His own righteousness and love have come, appealing to us through our human sympathies, that we too may be Sons. Here we have reached a truth which, I believe, shall not pass away so long as the soul thirsts for the living God. The forms of thought may change; the authorship of books may be uncertain; but when all else fails, the love of God which is in Christ Jesus our Lord will cool the fever of the heart, and make it feel the blessedness of a Father's presence. Not only through creation and through the voice of the Spirit in our conscience, but also through his Son

God will still reveal himself to those who wait for his salvation : and not with slavish subjection, but with the grateful joy of the redeemed, we will echo the ancient words: ' This is God's beloved Son; hear Him.'

X.

GOD AS LIGHT AND LOVE.

1 John i. 5.

' This then is the message which we have heard of him, and declare unto you, that God is light, and in Him is no darkness at all.'

1 John iv. 8.

' God is love.'

Such are the two propositions in which, with his characteristic union of artlessness and depth, the writer of this epistle sums up the revelation of God in Christ. Notwithstanding the opening verses of the Gospel, I think it may be safely said that John does not deal with the questions which are agitated in a speculative philosophy, but always keeps in view the relation of the truth which he announces to human life and its practical duties. The revelation of God, for which he thirsted, and which for the mass of men he considered the most necessary, was not one which allayed all the difficulties of the intellect, or satisfied our curious quest of knowledge, but one which bore upon the trials of the heart and conscience, and tended to make life more divine; and each manifestation of God's Spirit he regarded as the basis for some form of character in us. Following this method, in considering the revelation of God, we shall inevitably view at the same time its working in the human soul, and shall avoid all discussions relating to the mode of his existence and the internal economy of his nature, which, however interesting and useful in their proper place, belong rather to the chair of the philosopher than the pulpit of the Christian preacher. Practical truth, which may dwell as a power and a guide within the soul, is what Christianity would impart.

Let us turn our attention, then, to the statement contained in our first text, that 'God is light.' The expression is evidently figurative, and the precise meaning intended to be conveyed by it is nowhere defined. We may, however, gather its signification from the thoughts which follow; and the figure itself naturally suggests to the mind certain spiritual qualities. If we seek to understand it by the character of Christ, who is compared to a beam of the divine glory, we shall refer it to his luminous purity, his transparent candour, and his enlightened impartiality. Under this threefold aspect, we may consider the word in its application to God.

When we declare that 'God is light, and in Him

is no darkness at all,' we affirm that he is absolutely
holy, and that the splendour of his righteousness is
traversed by no dark lines of wrong-doing. This is
a truth which we readily accept; but its revelation
in our hearts is more than the intellectual acceptance
of it. It consists in a clear apprehension of an ideal
law, to which the Divine character is conformed; a
perception of what that holiness is in whose en-
folding presence we ever live. To speak of God as
supremely good, and then ascribe to him unworthy
actions, or to feel as little reverential awe when we
address him as if we were approaching an equal, is
merely to use flattering words, and prove that we
have never seen the light of that sanctity which the
highest angels must adore with fear and trembling.
He, then, who would reveal it must flash its brightness
into our souls, and make us feel what it is to stand
in presence of the infinitely Holy God, our Creator
and our Judge. And how could any one reveal
it, except as Christ has revealed it, by enshrining in
himself the spirit of holiness, and within the shadows
and limitations of our mortal lot making manifest
'the righteousness of God,' through a life of un-
blemished faithfulness to his will? The sinless
purity of Christ, that beam caught by him from the
eternal splendour, has flung its radiance over the
world; and wherever he has found a heart to dwell
in, he has impressed on that heart a new sense of
the Divine holiness, and filled with a new power its

conviction that 'God is light, and in Him is no darkness at all.' Now this revelation lies at the very basis
of the Christian life ; for it shows us for the first time
our need of a Christian life, our need of change, or
at least renewal, of our inward being. In discover-
ing the holiness of God, we discover at the same
time how estranged we are from that Father with
whom we would be in communion. The dawning of
His light in our souls makes us conscious of our
own darkness, and discloses many an unclean corner
where guilty passions and rebellious determinations
lurked. Conscience will accept no more the world's
idle apologies, but, stinging into life the sense of sin,
shows us as a chaos the character which our vanity
had surveyed as a paradise of beauty. And throughout our Christian course the light within serves to
make us aware of the darkness that yet remains;
and if we ever say in our hearts, that we have no sin,
it is not because our lives are so good, but because
we are so far from the light of God. This revelation
of our sin, too, is made with startling clearness by
Christ; for who, like him, has stirred our aspirations
for communion with God? Who has so brought
home to us the possibility, and with the possibility
the distance of a perfectly holy life ? And when do
we feel so bitterly our own weakness and shame, as
when we place ourselves beneath his cross and look
upon his saintly obedience and love? Thus through
him the Divine Holiness shines into our hearts, and

makes us conscious how unworthy are those temples
which it would claim for itself.

Again, as light is that which makes manifest,
when we speak of God as light, we cannot but think
of his perfect truthfulness, by virtue of which he
sees things exactly as they are, and, misled by no
hypocritical professions, blinded by no hollow disguises, searches the heart, and judges it according
to its real state. This, again, is a doctrine easy to
admit. That the judgment of God must be according to truth, is a statement which we cannot but
believe when presented in its abstract form; but did
it shine more brightly in our souls, it would possess
far greater practical power. Intellectually received,
we toss it away as a thing of no moment, and banish
to a distant and unknown future the solemn verdict
of Heaven upon our conduct; and we do not feel
what it is to have this judgment passed upon us
day by day, and hour by hour, and to have the
darkest and most secret windings of self-deception
tracked out and illumined by a Judge who cannot
err. This is what we need to have revealed, made
plain to the heart and conscience; and do we not
realise it more fully when we see the power with
which Christ unmasked hypocrisy and disentangled
the subtleties of self-love? Every character which
partakes of the simplicity and clearness of the Divine
light brings this truth nearer to us; and when we
place ourselves before the single-minded and in-

corruptible truthfulness of Christ, we feel uneasy under the self-interested arguments which before had satisfied us, our disguises drop away, and we become aware that within us the Supreme Judge holds his court, and pronounces his decisions through the oft-unheeded voice of conscience. This revelation in us, if it bear its proper fruit, leads to confession, a frank acknowledgment that we have sinned. So long as this is withheld, we are resisting the light, we are at enmity with God, and therefore can have no sense of His peace in our hearts. Pleasure, gaiety, we may have, but not the holy calmness of a spirit at one with God. We may tell ourselves and others that we have acted rightly; but a voice within will accuse our insincerity; and becoming enraged when we ought to be submissive, we shall substitute loud and angry asseveration for the modest dignity of conscious rectitude. But confession, flowing from the humbled and repentant heart, restores our peace, not only because it is itself a becoming act, but because it is a return to communion with God, an entrance once more into his light, and a participation in the truthfulness of his judgment. If therefore we seek that communion with the Father and the Son in which our real life consists, and rightly apprehend the message that 'God is light, and in Him is no darkness at all,' neither will there be in us the darkness of concealment; but laying down our pride, and desiring for ourselves no glory but to 'walk in the light as he is in the light,' we shall confess to him every unworthy act; and, so confessing, we shall find him 'faithful and just to forgive us our sins, and to cleanse us from all unrighteousness.'

Closely connected with the preceding is another thought, which leads, however, to practical conclusions of a widely different order. If God be light, he must be absolutely impartial; for partiality is a kind of darkness, a closing of the eyes against the truth, under the bias of self-interest or prejudice. All those distinctions, therefore, which depend upon national or ecclesiastical peculiarities must fail to obtain any recognition from Him. All peoples, all Churches, are held under one equitable survey, embraced by the same love, judged by the same righteousness, assigned their various gifts and duties by Him who rules the destinies of the world. We shall not consider this any far-fetched deduction from the Christian doctrine, when we remember that Jesus taught Samaritan and Jew to love one another, and that one of the earliest results of his life was the removal of the distinction between Jew and Gentile, and the union of both in the bonds of one spirit as children of the same Father. What, then, becomes of the self-righteous zeal of ecclesiastics and sectaries? what of the contemptuous pride and domineering insolence of powerful nations? The same holy Light is over them all, discriminating

with impartial exactness the evil and the good of
each.   God is no respecter of persons, of parties, or
of nations.   In every people he that feareth him,
and worketh righteousness, is accepted of him ; and
the only distinction recognised in the administration
of his justice is this—of those to whom he has committed much he demands the more.   This truth may
appear evident to our reason, but there is none
which we are so slow to receive in all the breadth of
its practical application.   With the tardy advent of a
polar sunrise, it is gradually stealing into the long
chill night of our prejudice.   We are beginning to
see that the estrangements on which men have
prided themselves, the persecutions which they have
conducted, the exclusive privileges which they have
appropriated, and the sanguinary wars which they
have waged, are but a sign of the darkness of the
human soul, and its distance from that God whom,
with a sort of perverted conscientiousness, it sought
to honour.   Under the light of a higher and nobler
faith, the strong are beginning to respect the rights
of the weak, the hand of oppression is struck down,
larger liberties are being conceded, and the false
distinctions created by religious or political pride
are melting like mists before the beams of the orient
sun.   Men of small minds or of small hearts, whose
bewildering self-interest or dim and affrighted
imaginations can see, even in the paradise of universal justice and love, nothing but shapes of horror

and ghastly visions of destruction and despair, will doubtless seek to prolong the reign of darkness, and petulantly cry, that they are the special favourites and chosen champions of God; but the truth that there is one God and Father of ALL shall yet be revealed in its glory, and the mind of man, caught up into communion with Him who is light, and in whom is no darkness at all, and so escaping from the blindness of habit, and the illusions of self-love, shall learn to see itself and all things in the light of Divine impartiality and justice.

We must now turn to the other portion of the Christian revelation of God, namely, the doctrine that 'God is love.' This doctrine admits of such numerous applications that it would be impossible to exhibit them at present; and I must confine myself to a few hasty suggestions, in pursuance of the line of thought already adopted. In relation to this doctrine, as in regard to the others of which I have spoken, what we need is, to have the reality and the meaning of Divine love brought home to our hearts. And who has ever revealed it to us as Christ has done? For he not only told us of it, but the Divine love lived and breathed in him, and through word and deed addressed its own appeal to the human soul. Christ filled this doctrine with a quickening power, and made men feel that the tender compassion of the Heavenly Father moved and worked in the midst of them; and many a cold and withered

heart, drooping under the oppression of its sin, or
cowed by the world's ruthless scorn, has revived
beneath the cross, and borne the blessed fruits of a
gracious and sanctified spirit, under the warming
assurance that it, too, is loved with an immeasurable,
all-sacrificing love. The meaning, also, of this love
has been shown by him. It was not to confer any
perishing good upon man, but to save him from the
dominion of sin, and kindle into life those spiritual
endowments which are his birthright, that Christ
toiled and died. So neither is the love of God
chiefly displayed in ministering to our selfish
pleasure, though for this, too, he makes most boun-
tiful provision, but in communicating some measure
of his own Spirit, and forming us into his own
image. The message of the Gospel is this, ' Behold
what manner of love the Father hath bestowed upon
us, that we should be called the children of God ; '
for we have not even glanced into the depths of
Divine love till we understand the majesty of this
title, and perceive that there is nothing greater
which love can possibly confer than this gift of
Sonship. But what if we have forfeited the name
and spurned the holy gift ? Is there yet hope ?
Yes ; for God's love does not weary, his invitation is
never withdrawn. ' There is forgiveness with him ; '
and when, having once seen our distant home, we
sigh like weary and baffled travellers, or even sit
down in despair at our own folly and guilt, no

sooner do we turn our faces towards him, and cry in our shame, ' We are no more worthy to be called Thy sons,' than he is at our side, and whispers to each fainting heart, ' My child, thy sins are forgiven thee ; trust not in thyself, but in ME, and all shall yet be well.' Nay, he even comes to entreat our stubborn temper, to seek and save the lost. From the deep fountains of his own Being his goodness flows, unpurchased, undeserved. From Him comes every capability we possess, the aspiration which lifts us towards him, the faith which assures us of his presence, the devotion which bows us in prayer ; from Him the call to holiness sounding through saint and prophet ; from Him the reconciling love of Christ, the soul-subduing power of the cross. How fervently, then, ought we to love Him who has thus loved us ; how earnestly should we endeavour to maintain that communion which He grants us ! Knowing that He is love, we ought to walk in love, and manifest His spirit towards all his creatures. Till that spirit abide in us, we have not found our true life. If we say that we are in the light, and hate our brother, or wilfully act unjustly or selfishly, we make the foolish boast of the hypocritical or the ignorant. The false trusts of correct belief, or ceremonial observance, or worldly wisdom, drop away before this simple test. Our Father is light and love ; we too, at least in the main direction of our thoughts and actions, must be light and love, or we are not his. I say, in the main direction of our lives, for, till the lesson of humility be fully learned, many a thick jet of darkness from the lower world of untamed and selfish passion will shoot athwart our path, and make our communion fitful; but still our faces may be turned heavenward, and the divine life, though engaged in conflict with baser elements, may be a reality, and destined to be a conquering power in our souls. Brightly and more brightly may the truth be revealed in our hearts; in more copious stream may the Spirit of sonship be poured upon us from on high; and at last, cleansed from all sin, may we be welcomed into our Father's eternal kingdom of light and love!

XI.

GOD AS THE AUTHOR OF LAW.

1 Corinthians xiv. 33.

' God is not the author of confusion, but of peace.'

In considering, in my last discourse, the revelation
of God in Christ, I remarked upon the two grand
Christian principles, that ' God is light ' and that
' God is love,' and endeavoured very briefly to indicate how these principles are, through Christ,
brought home to our hearts as significant and living
truths. To-day I would ask your attention to
another principle, which is stated in our text, ' God
is not the author of confusion, but of peace.' The
word *author*, as you will observe, from the italics
in which it is printed, has been inserted by our
translators, in order to complete the sense; and the
original expresses perhaps more clearly the intrinsic
nature of God, and might be rendered, ' God is not
a God of instability or anarchy, but of peace.' It
is important, in order to justify one or two applications which I shall venture to give to these words,

to remember the purpose for which they were
written. The Apostle is now seeking, not to control
the angry and factious spirit which prevailed in the
Church at Corinth, but to show the necessity for
observing order and rule in the conduct of public
services. Injudicious zeal, amounting sometimes
to fanatical and incoherent fervour, animated the
several speakers in the Church. The Apostle insists
on the necessity of controlling these outbursts of
enthusiasm, and doing all things 'decently and in
order,' and, among other reasons, urges the consideration that God, communion with whom, we must
remember, is the Christian life, 'is not a God of
anarchy, but of peace.'

If we ask how the nature of this peace is revealed
in Christ, we are at once reminded that we use as
almost synonymous expressions, 'the peace of
Christ' and 'the peace of God.' The former, as
having appeared in human history, and so riveted
the attention of men, takes priority in our thought;
but in accordance with the view, that he that hath
seen the Son hath seen the Father, it carries us
immediately to the peace of God, which is prior in
reality, for the filial peace of Christ is but the
peace of God abiding in him. Now, when we
observe the mind of Christ, what is the nature of
the peace which we there find? Does it not consist
in the prevalence of law or order? All his faculties
work in harmony. There is no fierce conflict of the
lower against the higher; but there is a becoming

subordination among the several powers, and each
contributes its own just measure to the impression
produced by his whole character. There is no rebellion, anarchy, or confusion, but the serenity of
forces all working with the most unselfish regularity
towards the same end. It is probably for this
reason that St. Paul, the great opponent of merely
legal observances, yet speaks of the ' *law* of the
Spirit of life in Christ Jesus,' and maintains that,
though he would abrogate the outward restraints of
the Mosaic Code, yet he would thereby establish
the reign of Law, for the Spirit of Christ was
essentially a spirit of order and conformity to the
highest rule of righteousness and truth. Carrying
up this thought to the Divine nature, must we not
admit that there too order prevails, that God is
indeed the fountain of Law, and, doing nothing
capriciously or incoherently, directs all his operations by the unvarying rule of the highest wisdom
and goodness?

The true application of this principle to the constitution of the Christian Church is not at first sight
obvious. The Church ought to be distinguished by
the prevalence of order and peace, and never to be
torn by schism, revolution, or confusion. But when
we ask how this result is to be secured, two widely
divergent answers may be returned. On the one
hand, it may be urged that this idea can be realised
only through the intervention of a hierarchical

K

system, in which the law shall be pronounced by one central authority, and exact unconditional and unreasoning obedience from all inferior members of the Church ; and that the unity of Christendom can have no intelligible meaning except in the combination of all Christian people under one visible organisation. This is the position of the Roman Church —a position grand in its conception, calculated to inflame the imagination, and serve as a ground for some of the loftiest, the widest, and most benevolent aspirations of our nature, and maintained in past times with a firmness, a daring, and a versatility of resource which are truly wonderful. And yet this system, based upon law, inculcating respect for authority as a fundamental duty, has produced the very schism and confusion which it was intended to prevent. As might have been foretold by those who possessed the writings of St. Paul, the system of outward restraint has become an intolerable yoke to the noblest spirits, not because they are averse to obedience, not because, with self-willed presumption, they choose their own way and have no desire to be led by a higher wisdom and goodness, but because there is a more binding law than the law of any Church, a more imperative restraint than the rule of even the most magnificent of earthly organisations.

There is then another way in which the Church may resemble its founder in breathing a spirit of order and peace. This other way has generally

been called individualism, a principle which, probably
from a misunderstanding of its true nature, there has
recently been some tendency to disparage among
those who ought to be its most consistent defenders.
By individualism, I do not mean the principle that
we are all to live, as it were, out of our own
centres, without mutual influence, mutual deference,
or even mutual submission, but that each man is
under a solemn obligation before God to follow the
light of his own conscience and reason, and that
therefore he ought to be left absolutely free to
follow it, and to determine for himself the limits of
his communion with others, in modes of belief, forms
of worship, or plans of benevolent activity. Specious
objections may be urged against this principle; but
they can have no weight with any one who holds it.
From the moment it enters the mind, it remains
there with the tenacity of a first truth. He who is
once convinced that in his own conscience and reason
he listens to the nearest word of God that it is
possible for him at the moment to hear, can only
reply to all objectors, ' I ought to obey God rather
than man.' He cannot renounce or profess to
renounce his belief because he is ordered to do so;
he cannot deny his conscience without appearing
guilty and ashamed before his Judge. This, however, is not saying that our conscience and reason
are infallible, or do not require the most careful
cultivation, or that it will do to consult them with-

out the profoundest reverence for righteousness and truth, or without the most candid readiness to acknowledge their limitation and feebleness, but only that, when upon consideration of the whole case their verdict is pronounced, that constitutes for us, for the time being, the supreme authority—an authority which we cannot disobey without being self-condemned and sunk in the humiliation of the only real infidelity. Humility will render us open to a change of view, on the presentation of further evidence; but till our judgment is altered by valid reasons, till our conscience is illumined with a purer light, we owe to our present convictions an absolute and unhesitating allegiance. If it be said that this principle, far from conducing to peace, will give rise to all sorts of eccentricity and confusion, I would, in reply, point to science, where this principle is truly recognised and honoured, and ask you whether Science—with her robe untorn by factions, with her calm and passionless worship of truth, and her lowly consciousness of her uncertainties and limitations, as well as of her conquests—is not far more like a daughter of Him who ' is not the author of confusion, but of peace,' than the Church, with her alienated sects, her self-righteous denunciations, and contradictory opinions, all maintained with the fierce pride of an assumed infallibility. Give to religion the same freedom which you have given to science; abjure sects, and worship truth; honour reason and conscience in others as you honour them in yourself; adore justice as the divine peace-maker; and the Church will again be clothed in the seamless vesture of Christ, discover that the spiritual, like the natural laws of God, require an infinite variety of manifestation, and, coveting no more to be an earthly monarch, will rest with devout joy in the blessed ' unity of the Spirit,' and so prove herself—what the sense of guilt might prevent her claiming to be at present— the offspring of Him who ' is not the author of confusion, but of peace.'

There is another application of the principle with which we started. As in the Church order ought to prevail through the operation of the Divine law in the hearts of its several members, so we might expect that in the physical world, with its various modes of force and the infinite multiplicity of forms through which that force manifests itself, the supremacy of Law would abolish all capricious and unconnected action, constrain each part with unconscious self-denial to minister to the universal good, and so produce an orderly result. It seems strange that science, which so completely demonstrates the correctness of this expectation, and in every department so exquisitely illustrates the Christian truth, that ' God is not the author of confusion, but of peace,' should not only arouse the jealousy of a few narrow theologians, but should excite in many religious minds vague apprehensions, as though

God were about to be dethroned by the very perfection of his own arrangements.

In professed theological circles suspicions are awakened by the fact that some of the discoveries of science are in distinct opposition to some long-cherished dogmas, with which religion has been so intimately associated that it is supposed they must stand or fall together. For instance, every scientific man whose opinion is worth having is confident that the world was not created in six days, about six thousand years ago. This fact is clearly opposed to the doctrine of the infallibility of the Bible, on which Protestantism, with more zeal than either discretion or insight, has based religion; and therefore the very simple and reasonable proposition, that the writer of the first chapter of Genesis, however imbued with the Spirit of God, was not familiar with the truths which modern science has explored, appears to sound the knell of man's religious hopes.

But the temporary chill which science appears to have thrown over religion is due, I think, to more than this distinct conflict between old dogma and new truth. In many minds which have no distaste for science and no disinclination to accept its discoveries, there is an uneasy feeling, hardly confessed even to themselves, that Law is gradually taking the place of God, and that when the whole universe is shown to be under its control, no room

will be left for the Divine operation. It was, till
a recent period, customary to retreat from the
present dominion of law, and appeal to the existence of creative epochs, in which, it was urged, the
Divine power must have stepped in, as the old laws
were inadequate to produce the new results. But
now creative epochs are melting away under the
magic wand of science; development, extending
over millions of years, is solving the mystery of
species; and there is a law by which, if only you
allow sufficient time for each successive change to
be imperceptibly minute, the highest forms of being
may be evolved from the lowest. But why should
all this affect our religion, except to awaken a
profounder reverence, a more awe-struck adoration?
for the universe has enlarged its seeming limits, and
our thought is lost in the vastness of its periods
and the stupendous grandeur of its works. It is as
though a cloud, which gave portentous dimensions
to the neighbouring rocks and bushes dimly loom-
ing through, had suddenly dispersed and shown us
the real magnificence of the scene—dizzy precipice,
dark and stormy pass, and mountain piled on mountain, and stretching away and away till eyesight
can reach no further, and the mind is overwhelmed
with the glory of the prospect.

The difficulty which is felt arises, I believe, not
at all from the real drift of the evidence, but
largely from a mere habit of speech. We speak

of a law as though it were a real thing, capable of doing something. A form of theology has prevailed which has been content with this view, and even insisted upon it. It has been conceded that where natural laws can be shown to prevail there is no occasion to assume the Divine activity; and conclusive evidence of God's presence has been sought in his occasional 'interference' with these laws, and in his 'overruling' them, as though they were distinct forces, capable of doing their own work independently of Him. Starting from such a view, we may well ask, if law is now shown to be universal, will it not account for everything? and why, then, should we assume the existence of God? The answer is, that a law can do nothing and explains nothing. That we should ascribe to it any such power arises from the mere indolence of habit. That which has always happened we take for granted must happen through a sort of natural necessity; but the moment we ask ourselves what natural necessity can mean, and why it is that the occurrence happens, we are furnished with no answer but the old one, that it is the effect of some invisible will. Admit the existence of God, and we have an adequate explanation of the universe; deny it, and there is no opposing theory; we are then in absolute ignorance of the cause of this strangely beautiful world, apparently so marvellously designed, governed with such unity of plan, and tending to the fulfilment of so grand a moral purpose. For a law is but the generalised statement of what actually occurs, informing you of a fact, but withholding the reason and the cause. Accept the Divine Will as the cause, and then natural laws express the modes of operation of that Will, and all the exquisite processes that go on around us daily become the tokens of his living power, while the uniformity of their action reveals his unwearied constancy. Reason and will are the fountains of order. The supremacy of Law is a sign, therefore, not of their absence, but of their presence; and when you point to the physical world as the sphere of Law, and demonstrate the stability, the harmony and the peace of its operations, you afford a splendid confirmation of the truth of the apostolic words, 'God is not the author of confusion, but of peace.'

We must for a moment glance at one other application of our principle. If the influence of God's Spirit produces order and unity in the Church, if his creative power proceeds by determinate methods which make the universe the domain of Law, are we to suppose that his action in the soul can be capricious and unstable? or shall we not rather expect that his grace will descend with the same regularity, and with the same conformity to fixed conditions, as the sunshine and rain? The laws which regulate

the communion of the soul with God may indeed
be more subtle and less capable of exact expression
than the laws of nature. Yet there are some laws
confirmed by all religious experience, and admitting
of clear statement, such as these—that God withholds
the blissful consciousness of his presence from those
who obstinately cherish unrepented guilt, that he
restores his peace to the heart of the truly penitent,
that the man who trusts in Him is blessed, that the
pure in heart shall see him. Acknowledging the
reality of such laws, may we not carry our thought
farther, and believe that here, too, the presence of
Law is the surest sign of God's activity, and that all
the benign and beautiful influences which help to
mould our characters, whether arising in the exercise
of our own minds or occurring in our intercourse with
friends, are evidence at once of his living power in
our souls and his paternal interest in our spiritual
growth? Here, too, much needless scepticism has
arisen from our habit of looking for God in the
exceptional and lawless, rather than in the usual and
normal. We think that he does not speak to us,
because his Word is not a violent breaking in of a
supernatural voice, in violation of our mental laws;
and instead of accepting the perennial faithfulness of
conscience as the everliving action of His Spirit, we
refer it to our natural constitution, and think that we
have thereby eliminated God. I would not indeed
deny that the soul has its Pentecostal days, as nature

has its earthquakes, its storms, and its lightnings,
and that these more vividly excite our drowsy
apprehensions, and may startle us for the first time
from the deathly dream of sense into the perception
of the awful Holiness, the unfathomable Wisdom,
and the all-embracing Love in the midst of which
we live; and there is some excuse if we occasionally
dwell upon these as the times when God was indeed
present with us, and disturbed with a blessed confusion the routine of an unregenerate nature.   But
as the lightning has its law, so doubtless have these
explosive manifestations of spiritual fervour, and
God is no less present in our quiet and equable
growth in faith, righteousness, and love. The truths
that often stray through our minds, the aspirations that arise we know not how, the deepening
of holy thought through reverent meditation, the
brightening of the path of duty by submissively
taking our cross, the calmness which steals over the
heart in the house of prayer, the feelings of penitence or humility, or comfort, or devout gladness
kindled by reading or listening to the words of
another—all these, natural as we call them, are the
traces of God's Spirit in our hearts.   Oh, may we
learn thus to own him day by day, and to seek him,
where he ever dwells, within the realm of Law, im-
pressing his own beauty, stability, and order upon
all that does not resist his Will!   And let us trust
ourselves fearlessly to Him, though he should lead

us by untrodden paths, and not dread anarchy in
the world of thought, in religion, or in the State as
the result of humble submission to his laws ; for in
the Church, in material creation, and in the soul,
‘ He is not the author of confusion, but of peace.’

XII.

THE SENSE OF SIN TOUCHED BY THE REVELATION OF GOD.

Job xlii. 5, 6.

'*I have heard of thee by the hearing of the ear : but now mine eye seeth thee. Wherefore I abhor myself, and repent in dust and ashes.*'

These words express with the utmost simplicity, and at the same time with remarkable depth, the difference between information about God received from others and the revelation of him in our own souls, and also the difference between the spiritual results of these two modes of knowledge.

In treating, some time ago, of the subject of revelation, I endeavoured to show that it consists essentially in the opening of the spiritual eye, in the clear inward apprehension of the reality and the meaning of Divine things through our own religious experience. It is, as St. Paul says, an enlightening of the eyes of the heart, a taking away of the veil from the heart, a shining of the Divine Spirit within the conscience. He who can merely inform us about God, and convey to us some true statements about his character and providence, may be a wise teacher, but is not a revealer; he alone reveals God who increases our spiritual sensibility, and rends the veil that hangs before the Holy of Holies at the centre of our own being. How beautifully is this expressed, without any thought of enunciating a theological theory, in the simple utterance of the soul's experience : ' I have heard of thee by the hearing of the ear; but now mine eye seeth thee!' Job had been a devout man, faithful in the discharge of every duty which piety and benevolence required : he is described as ' a perfect and an upright man, one that feareth God and escheweth evil;' and yet he had not attained to the deepest and grandest experience that is open to the human soul. His knowledge of God had been the result of hearsay, gathered from the thoughts of the wise or the instructions of his elders, but not lighted up by any radiance shining from within. This knowledge, however, is not to be lightly spoken of. It may be that it is the highest to which most men attain; and when received by a simple and noble-minded man, it was sufficient to produce a lofty type of character, and to create in suffering a trustful patience which has become proverbial. Yet when the deeper fountains of Job's life had been broken up by affliction, and his enlarging experience struggled against the cramping limits of the old theology which he had learned by the hearing of the ear,

God seemed to come to him no longer through the imperfect words of others, but to visit his own soul, and to speak truth directly to his own heart. He passed into that immediate personal relation to God which is the highest religion; and in comparison with his present vision of the Divine majesty, his former life, though he had been able justly to reflect upon it with so much satisfaction, appeared a life remote from God, in which he had known him by rumour, not by sight. Through much tribulation he had entered into the kingdom of God, and the King was at last revealed in his glory.

What, then, was the first effect of this revelation of God? It brought with it to Job a revelation of himself—'Wherefore I abhor myself, and repent in dust and ashes.' Seeing himself in the light of human opinion, and seeing himself in the light of God, were two very different things. In the former he was the high-minded, generous, and religious man, and was able to repel with indignant consciousness of rectitude the extravagant charges of his friends; but in the latter he was the frail mortal, with sins to repent and shortcomings to bewail, and unprepared with any reply to Him whose judgment is according to truth. Even his soul could not bear to be illumined by the burning rays of the Divine holiness; and when, in the profound consciousness of a higher Presence, he forgot alike the applause and the reproaches of the world, and seemed to stand alone before God, he had room only for feelings of self-abhorrence and contrition.   Thus it always is.   Our self-complacency can exist only while God still seems at a distance from us, while the immeasurable extent of our obligations to Him is still hidden, and we know him only by the hearing of the ear; as soon as his righteous judgment reveals itself in our own souls, and he becomes to us the one great Reality in whose presence all the vanity of the world's opinion disappears, and we stand face to face with him in the solitude of our hearts, we too are touched with the sense of sin; in finding Him we find for the first time our real selves, and would bow our repentant spirits in the dust.

If this view be correct, it must follow that he who most clearly reveals God also probes most deeply the consciousness of sin; and if it be true, as I have endeavoured to show on a previous occasion, that in seeing Christ we see the Father, we may expect the sense of sin to be a predominant Christian sentiment, and the deliverance of man from sin to be one of the great concerns of the Christian Church.

In seeking to unfold the Christian view of this subject, let me say, once for all, at starting, that while I may claim for the Christian revelation a marked pre-eminence, I have no wish to assert its exclusiveness.   The book of Job itself furnishes an instance of another kind of revelation; for though Job himself may not have been a real person, yet the religious experiences described in the book must have been real and familiar to its author. Now the revelation of God, with its accompanying sense of sin, is represented as having come to Job through meditation on the wonderful works of nature, aided by the increased sensibility imparted by pain and sorrow. While, then, in our own or in the world's history we admit that the profoundest impression for good has been produced by Jesus Christ, we must not ungratefully forget how much we owe to the magnificent creation amid which we are placed, and to the varied discipline of our lives, or how often our susceptibility to Christ's influence is itself awakened by something outside the direct stream of his agency. The revelation of himself in Christ is, in my belief, the grandest, but yet only one of the many grand approaches by which God seeks admittance to our hearts. With this caution, let us view the sense of sin in its Christian aspect.

However it may be explained, and however subtle abstract objections may be taken to the possibility of Christ's moral perfection, it will hardly be denied that he has left upon the world an impression of transcendent holiness and goodness. So far did these surpass the ordinary life of man, so completely did they seem to realise the brightest prophetic dreams, that the early disciples could describe them only as the Spirit of God, the complete indwelling of the Divine Word, the mani-

L

festation upon earth of the eternal life of the Father.
Men appeared to have been visited by the awful
Sanctity to which they must render an account,
and to have beheld for a moment upon the stage of
human history that Goodness which at all times
encircles them unseen.   A quickened sense of
responsibility, a new conviction of the certainty of
judgment, a deeper insight into the Divine character, were the inevitable result.   The impulse that
made Peter exclaim, ' Depart from me, for I am a
sinful man, O Lord,' shows us the power by which
Christ's Spirit pierced the conscience; and Peter's
was no solitary case, for wherever the light of that
Spirit fell, it led men to abhor themselves and repent in dust and ashes. This power, with which Christ
appeals to the conscience, is heightened by the fact
that in him we see the Divine Spirit, not only as
Divine, but as human; not only as existing in the
inaccessible glory of the Father, but as dwelling in
communion with the life of man; not only as the
high and fearful holiness by which we shall be
judged, but as the lowly and submissive self-consecration by which we ought to live.   We understand
the meaning of the life of God in the soul.   We
become aware that these corruptible bodies may be
temples of the Holy Spirit; that these members, so
often the instruments of selfish passions, may be
organs of the Supreme Will.   We learn that we
may be Sons, living in and for God, with the beauty

of his peace, the grandeur of his purpose, the tenderness of his love abiding in our own bosoms. Is it strange that such a faith, kindled into living force by one in whom these things are realities, and not cold philosophic dreams, should create in us a sense of sin, and mingle the sighs of baffled aspiration with the songs of triumph in the Church? The glory of our vision reveals how dark and sad are many of the facts of life, and we can hardly bear to look from the cross into our own hearts. Having there seen for a moment behind the veil, we know henceforward what it is to be 'alienated from the life of God,' and become conscious of all the bitterness of our sin.

Hence we can understand how it is that the sense of unworthiness, and the conviction that his soul is not at peace with God, may fall with even a crushing weight upon one whom men, judging from the outside, would pronounce upright in all his dealings. It is that the fair outward seeming will no longer satisfy the high demands of conscience, and the self-delusion, which so often blinds us when all men speak well of us, has dispersed like a fog before the rising beams of the Divine Spirit. Others are unable to see the unconsecrated will, or the secret selfishness which poisons the fountains of our life. Others are unable to see the murmuring of the heart against God, the coldness of its gratitude and love, the feebleness of its sympathy with his

purposes. They can but roughly guess from a few
of our actions what is the dominant power within
us; but we ourselves can plunge beneath our actions,
and turn the light of God upon our hearts. We
may, in communion with Him, discover and mourn
each dark blot, or in the woful sense of broken
communion become aware that there must be some
deadly disease within. We may, then, claim that we
stand well with our fellow-men, and consider ourselves above their just reproach, and yet in our re-
tirement wrestle in close grasp with sin, and with
contrite tears implore that peace of God whose
touch we feel, but the fulness of whose fruition appears so distant still.

Does any one say that this describes a morbid
state of mind, one that preys upon its own fancies,
and is not alive to the broad practical bearings of life?
To me it seems to be the soul's awakening from a
feverish dream, and its calm impartial survey of
itself and all things in the light of eternal day, and
no longer through the bewildering mists of earth.
Morbid it may become, if unwisely treated, or if it
spring from mere selfish dread about our own salvation; but if it arise from God's revelation of
himself in the heart, it is the first symptom of returning health. The ends which self-love pursues
are the deceitful fancies which mock us even as we
embrace them, and which every man knows are
perishable, while after they have perished is the

judgment. But justice, truth, love, holiness, are the eternal things which never make ashamed, and which shall meet us when we stand, in terror or in trust, before the throne of God. It is well if we catch even now a vision of the glorious life of the Sons of God, and if out of the whirlwinds of our earthly existence God reveal himself to our souls, so that, like Job, we may murmur with mingled sorrow and hope, ' We have heard of thee by the hearing of the ear; but now our eyes see thee. Wherefore we abhor ourselves, and repent in dust and ashes.'

If we look more closely at the sense of sin awakened by the revelation of God, we find that it involves two elements, of which one may be comparatively transient, while the other accompanies us far upon our Christian course.

There is, in the first place, the sense of guilt, the consciousness of having made a wrong choice and deliberately lived for self rather than God. How little this is affected by the outward colouring of our life, it is easy to see. Our higher respectability may be simply the result of a more wary prudence ; and we may, through the force of habit or the influence of associates, be above the commission of crime, and yet have no real preference for righteousness and for God. The revelation of a Father, on whom we depend for all things, and who has an indefeasible right to our perfect obedience, generally finds us with this solemn choice still to be made. It shows us how we have permitted self-love to be our predominant motive, and how little the determination to live for God has given direction and tone to our conduct. Hence the necessity for what has been technically called conversion, which is simply the transference of our allegiance from self to God, the solemn and deliberate consecration of the will to his service. It is the most serious question that we can propose to ourselves, whether we have yet made that choice, whether we have resolved—with that humility which knows its own infirmity of purpose, with that wondering thankfulness which knows its own unworthiness of so blessed an invitation—that we will, through weal and woe, follow the leading of our Father. Till we can answer this question satisfactorily, we cannot have peace with God. Let us ask it in the silence of our souls, and pray for a true reply.

But our choice may have been made, and the sense of guilty defiance of the higher Will have passed away. When we have entered on the life with God, has the consciousness of sin been therefore slain, to rise and trouble us no more? No; we have girded on our armour, and committed ourselves to the battle; but our rest is not yet. The revelation of Divine love enshrined in a human heart shows us our own disordered passions and tumultuous desires, needing to be tamed and clad in the beauty of holiness. The actual stands out in contrast to the ideal; and these mortal bodies, which we would gladly yield as harmonious instruments to be touched by the breath of God, are sadly out of tune. With eager flush, we respond to the trumpet blast of passion, but, weary and uncertain, tremble at the 'still small voice' of the Spirit. The chains of evil habit must be unfastened, and the spell of our earthly nature broken; and though we may still be pressing on towards God, we cannot but be conscious of many things which are not in conformity with his Will. Till all our powers are brought into subjection to the obedience of Christ, and we ourselves are transfigured into the likeness of the Son of God, we shall not fully escape the oppression of moral evil or reach the goal of our aspiration. 'Be ye perfect, as your Father in Heaven is perfect,' is a rule which leaves no room for pride or self-gratulation; and though, with Job, we may have striven to live for God, yet with each more vivid revelation of Him we must abhor ourselves, and 'repent in dust and ashes.'

XIII.

INNOCENCE.

ROMANS vii. 9 (first part).

'*I was alive without the law once.*'

WHEN we treat of moral and spiritual states of
mind, it is necessary, for the sake of clearness, to
mark them off from one another in our thought by
much sharper distinctions than exist in fact. Thus
we are in the habit of dividing men into two classes,
which in our conception are very widely separated—
the bad and the good. But when we mingle among
actual men, the division seems almost to disappear.
There are, indeed, some to whom without hesitation
we ascribe the epithet bad, and others who are
as clearly entitled to the designation of good. But
between these there is a vast multitude of men possessing every imaginable shade of character, and
rendering it quite impossible to determine the line
of demarcation which in our own minds we had considered so unmistakeable.

There are some who suppose that, while the moral
distinction is thus incapable of any clear application

in the world of fact, men may with much more certainty be classified religiously. It seems a safe proposition that any given man either does or does not consciously and intentionally serve God, and that therefore mankind may be truly divided into those who serve God and those who are indifferent or hostile to him. But even here facts present the same doubtful aspect as in the case of the moral division. There are those whom we might naturally place in the ranks of the indifferent, who yet have stray feelings of devotion, and occasionally perform an action under a genuine religious impulse. And, on the other hand, there are not a few who have with all earnestness devoted themselves to God, who yet are guilty of acts of rebellion, and spend many an hour when their hearts are callous to religious influences. Here too our logical distinctions become evanescent; and though the two extremes are separated by a wide gulf, the space is bridged over by a long line of men, who stand in such close proximity that it is impossible to select any two who are beside one another, and justly assign them to different ranks.

This observation is hardly less true when applied to successive spiritual conditions of the same soul. There are undoubtedly many, more probably than we are at all aware of, who can divide their own life into two marked periods, and know the precise date when a complete change swept over their mind and heart. This change occurs not only in those who have lived in determined opposition to the laws of God, but in those who have striven, with more or less fidelity, to do their duty so far as they knew it, but to whom religion has presented itself only in its external aspect, who have been strangers to its deepest emotions, and never vividly felt their own personal relation to God. We need not go for illustration beyond the example of St. Paul. Though he was always conscientious, and in a certain sense religious, yet a spiritual change passed suddenly over him, which made him a different man. This is a clear instance, because (and this is not always the case) his outward life underwent as complete an alteration as his inward, and we find it difficult to recognise the same person in Saul the Jew and Paul the Christian. But we have no reason to believe that the change by which religion, from being far off and vague and impotent, becomes the nearest and most active power in the life, invariably occurs in this sudden and revolutionary manner. It is sometimes the result of silent growth, and the alteration becomes evident only by a comparison of distant years. In regard to other less radical changes of character, the various stages of our progress appear to melt into one another by imperceptible degrees. We cannot tell when the first notions of right and wrong faintly dawned upon the mind; when conscience, hitherto dormant, assumed its responsibility;

when evil habits were completely destroyed; when faith finally triumphed over doubt; when peace and love and holy joy became the familiar inmates of the soul. And his is the most beautiful and perfect character who from the child grows into the saint, unconscious of any spiritual convulsion, and simply fulfilling in each stage of his being the laws which God has appointed to regulate his progress.

We must bear these remarks in mind when we speak of spiritual conditions, and not expect to meet with the same clearly marked stages in the world of reality as in the world of thought. We may consider the nature of innocence in the abstract, although it is impossible to determine with accuracy in individual cases when innocence ceases and responsible life begins.

The state of innocence is that in which there is no knowledge of right and wrong. This is the position which we occupy before the development of character commences. It has pleased God that man should start on his career morally on the same level as the brutes, and gradually win his way upwards. At first he is impelled by simple instincts, making no distinction between the nobler and the less noble, but following that which for the moment happens to be most powerful. He is not conscious of the restraints of any law, but whatever nature prompts he does freely. In this condition he cannot sin, for sin is the intentional violation of a known rule. Where there is no law, there can be no transgression; and before conscience has grasped the idea of a better and a worse, no offence can be committed. There is therefore no self-reproach; and that consciousness of deserving a just penalty, or of falling far short of a clearly discerned ideal, which so often in later life flings a dark shadow across the natural brightness and cheerfulness of spirit, does not yet cloud the mind or disturb its serenity with violent compunctions.

It is this innocence, with its happy, careless gaiety, which gives such a charm to the life of the lower animals. It is delightful to see such multitudes of creatures enjoying themselves without care and without sin, sporting with the artless beauty of nature, and obeying with simple trust the instincts which a Divine hand has given them. When we watch the gambols of a kitten, it is not merely the grace and fun of its movements that gives us pleasure; it is its unalloyed happiness and its exuberance of life. Somewhat similar is the attractiveness of childhood. We do not there observe the dignity and the high pleasures of later years; but we see an unaffected grace and spontaneity of action, a redundancy of life, and a pure abandonment to the happiness of the moment, of which we detect but scanty traces in middle age. Lovely childhood, with its artless wiles, its unadulterated affections, its guileless merriment, seems fresh from the hand of God, and exults in the freedom of those who know not darkness, doubt, or sin. Very remarkable is the language of St. Paul, 'I was *alive* without the law once.' In comparison with rosy childhood, the hard struggle of the man, the flesh and spirit lusting against one another, the terrible rebukes of conscience, the vain aspirings, the bitter regrets, appeared like a kind of death. The chain of the law hung heavy upon every movement. Not an instinct could he gratify till the question was answered, Is it right? Not an effort could he make without feeling that he came short of the glory of God. The sentence of death was written black upon his heart, for never had he satisfied the awful holiness of conscience. The thought of childhood was a bright paradise of life and joy seen through the long dark vista of error, conflict, and disappointment. Though absolute innocence belongs only to infancy, yet, comparatively speaking, it remains far into childhood; and it is quite conceivable that Paul may have remembered the time when the law, with its severe demands and cumbrous observances, had not yet claimed its sovereignty over him; and the thought of merry romps with his mother or his sister, and of sunny rambles among the Cilician hills, may have lingered in his memory, more radiant perhaps with his own warm imagination, as a picture of happier days. And so the words, 'I was alive without the law once,' may have

represented a real fact in his mental history, and
awakened the far-off echoes of home, where he had
sported in boyish glee, conscious only of a parent's
smile and an overflowing energy of life.

With whatever sadness is contained in the words
of the Apostle many will be found to sympathise.
It is no uncommon thing to look back regretfully
to the innocence of childhood, and contrast it with
the onerous responsibilities of man's estate. It was
the golden time of life, when all was fresh and wonderful, when joy rose like a perennial spring, and
grief was but as the passing shower which renders
the air more balmy. Anxiety had not yet over-
shadowed the brow, nor the autumn tints of sorrow
given token of approaching winter. And if any
appearance of sin created a temporary gloom, it was
speedily forgotten in the sweetness of instant reconciliation. Who would not wish to experience once
more the free movement, the buoyant activity, the
indomitable hope, the pure admirations of early life,
and to exchange, for at least a day, his cares, his
fears, his concealments, his repented or unrepented
sins, for its unabashed frankness and rapturous
mirth? So prevalent is this feeling of melancholy,
in looking back to former days, that the world too is
represented as having had its golden age; and
ancient story tells us of a Paradise where all was
peace and love; and if the highest virtue and faith
were unknown, depravity, meanness, and doubt were

no less absent. Purity and gladness reigned in those Eden bowers; and the awful feeling of estrangement from a Father with whom we might be in communion had not yet, like a starless night, veiled the terrified heart. No broken tables of the law bore witness against the soul; no hater of his brother went out from the presence of the Lord, branded with an unbearable punishment. In comparison with that abode of innocence, earth has appeared like a dreary desert, a vale of tears, where every heart knows its own bitterness, and life is a weary struggle to regain what has been for ever lost. Imagination fondly lingers by those verdant banks where the first pair beguiled the happy hours, and in their tranquil bliss were hardly conscious of the lapse of time ; and it is with a sigh that we confront once more the broad realities of life.

Yet there is another side to this picture, and in forfeiting innocence our gain has been greater than our loss. Beautiful as the opening spring, the state of innocence lacks the ripening warmth of summer and the rich fruits of harvest-time. The young unsullied life is full of attractiveness, but it does not possess the elements of moral grandeur. Before the knowledge of right and wrong is awakened, there is no self-determining power, but, like the lower animals, we submissively follow the leading of instinct. We are not yet conscious of two opposing forces within us, one which we should like to gratify, the other which

we ought to obey. Passion has not been confronted
by conscience, and the will called upon to surrender
to a higher law than that of impulse or self-interest.
Hence we have still an unbroken peace within our
hearts, and have no idea of the fierce inner conflict
by which virtue must be won. But though this condition is a pleasant one, and though in some painful
or dreamy moments we look back regretfully, like
the Israelites, to the time when we had plenty of
animal comfort, and were not yet awakened by the
voice of the great Lawgiver to the ignominy of
serfdom, yet there is here nothing noble; and we do
not assume the distinctive greatness of human nature
till we face the burning desert, and meet our foes in
dread encounter, that we may reach at last a
promised land of freedom. If we have no battle,
neither can we have a victory; and no trophy will
rise to show the supremacy of the soul, unless we
measure our strength against the tempter. And not
only so, but without a knowledge of right and wrong,
and the power to choose between them, we could
make no spiritual progress. Intellectually, indeed,
we might advance, but we could come no nearer to
God. Never could we be his Sons, for his most
glorious attributes would be totally unknown. With
the wailing of remorse would expire too the fervent
cry of aspiration, the low breathings of gratitude for
undeserved mercies, the supplicating prayer for
deliverance, the humble vow of self-consecration.

Stagnation would reign with a weary uniformity over the whole surface of the spiritual being; and that which in the early dawn of our existence appears pre-eminently life would, when prolonged beyond its proper period, be found more akin to death, possessing no principle of growth, and exhibiting the same blank face from age to age. If, then, the state of innocence were perpetual, human history would be robbed of its grandest passages. All that is most fascinating in the history of man is connected with his power of moral choice. Without this, the solemn warnings of prophets would never have been spoken; the gradual corruption and terrible retribution of nations, with all their heart-rending details, would never have occurred; martyrs would never have been dragged to the stake, and proved, while the flame slowly consumed their limbs, that fidelity to truth is stronger than the torture of the bigot, and the righteousness of God mightier than the wrath of man. Never does the soul appear so grand as when, tempted, pained, despised, it nevertheless clings to the right which it reveres, and will not bow to any base idol of popular opinion or of passion which could separate it from the living God. We might perhaps go even beyond this, and say that the exhibitions of satanic power, a will daring to defy the Omnipotent and pursue its own course at every cost, have in them more sublimity than the blind acquiescence of the brutes. But a

M

soul which no pains can terrify, no pleasures seduce from the right; which deliberately prefers the Will of God to all else that the universe can offer; which presents a serene front when the ominous cry, 'Crucify him, crucify him!' bursts from a savage and deluded mob; which prays for its tormentors when the nails are being driven into the shrinking flesh, and trusts in God when the dimness of death creeps over the face still so young—this is a spectacle of grandeur and heroism which you look for in vain in a paradise of untempted innocence; and that one such soul has existed fills with significance all the struggles and tears that the world has known since the bloom of Eden faded into a tradition of the past. Cheerfully, then, let us accept our lot, and believe that the failures and stumblings, the sighs, the anxieties, and the darkness of the present are all incidents on an upward course, and in falling from pristine innocence we have entered on a path which more befits the dignity of immortal spirits; and, though we are conscious of clouds between us and God, we are nearer him than we were in childhood's hour, when we knew not that we must aspire endlessly towards him, and choose him as our supreme end.

To be 'alive without the law' is ours no more. But far away across the ages another more glorious life invites us. Conflict shall at last be over, and the simplicity of the saint replace the innocence of the child. Then our whole nature shall be consciously given to God; and his Spirit shall so pervade every part that all our emotions and desires, no less than our determined choice, will rise towards Him. The hardship of obedience shall be forgotten in the ecstasy of love. We shall be born of God, and caught up into such a high communion that sin can no more intrude. Then the spontaneous freedom and beauty of childhood will return, not now ignorant and incapable of self-direction, but crowned by the virtue, the wisdom, and the love of a victorious and glorified spirit. How far away this fulness of life may be, we know not. In part, it depends on the faithfulness of each soul. But from that sweet and pure and happy life which we enjoyed before the law was revealed in our conscience let us learn to picture that nobler life of the free children of God which we hope to attain. Meanwhile let us endure hardness as good soldiers of Jesus Christ, and know that He who raised his Son from the dead will also quicken his faithful followers.

XIV.

THE AWAKENING OF CONSCIENCE.

ROMANS vii. 9 (second part).

' When the commandment came, sin revived, and I died.'

WHEN the Apostle Paul·speaks absolutely of the
law, we can hardly doubt that he refers, primarily at
least, to the law of Moses. That was the law which
he had himself experienced; and the good or evil
results which flow from the authority of Law were
associated in his mind with the venerable institutions
of Judaism. Moral precepts naturally shaped themselves into the words of the Ten Commandments, and
ritual observances conformed to the Israelitish type.
From the general course of his argument, however,
it is difficult to avoid the conclusion, that he regarded
the Mosaic Code as only the embodiment of a more
universal law. He speaks of Gentiles fulfilling the
requirements of the law under the guidance of nature, and so being a law to themselves. Several of
his reasonings are quite as applicable to the abstract
idea of a moral law as to that special form of it with

which he was most familiar. And where he vindi-
cates himself from the charge of making void the
law, and maintains that, on the contrary, he establishes it, his words seem hardly intelligible if we
confine their meaning to the institutes of Moses.
He had been arguing that by works of the law none
could be justified, that the new principle, which he
calls 'faith,' could alone render man acceptable to
God; this was all-sufficient and was quite independent of the law. But then arose the objection, You
are introducing a lawless condition, and men freed
from control will abandon themselves without scruple
to sin. No, replied the Apostle, we are simply
placing the moral order of the world upon a new and
higher basis, and securing more powerful sanctions
for the maintenance of that order. There is a law
of faith as well as a law of works; and in insisting
that the Mosaic law has completed its purpose, and
must no longer be binding on the conscience, instead
of introducing confusion, we are establishing the
dominion of law. Thus we seem justified by St.
Paul's own use of the word in extending its meaning beyond the special instance, and giving to his
reasoning on the subject a more universal application.

To each of us the Law comes when the knowledge
of right and wrong enters the mind. We are not
destined to remain in a condition of happy innocence,
doing without restraint whatever the passing moment

suggests.   Sooner or later, we learn that we are
under a rule by which our actions ought to be guided.
The reign of impulse is over; or if we thoughtlessly
yield to mere ebullitions of feeling, we smart under
a stern protest from the newly-discovered law.   We
may no longer do whatever occurs to our mind as
pleasant, but we must bring every word and deed
for judgment before the supreme tribunal which has
been erected within us.   The moral law claims
authority over every part of our life.   It is an omni-
present power, and speaks in imperative and un-
adorned language, ' Thou shalt do this; thou shalt
not do that.'   It does not condescend to reason with
us, or to make its commandments attractive.   It
simply requires our obedience, and terrible is its lash
if we disobey.   It may be that in actual life this
severe authority of conscience seldom reigns alone,
unattended by any ministers of milder aspect.   There
are usually periods when it seems to have de-
scended from the judgment-seat, and to have left us
once more to the free movements of instinctive life;
or we catch glimpses of a Spirit ' full of grace and
truth,' which belongs to a higher region than the
law, and for a moment obedience loses all its harsh
and repulsive character.   The time too may be impossible to determine with accuracy when the knowledge of right and wrong first steals into the mind;
and that knowledge may possess every variety of
clearness in different persons.   Still we can under-

stand with sufficient distinctness the state of mind in which conscience presents itself as a bare law, and what obedience we render to it is a pure act of submission to its dictates. Duty is certainly not always attractive; nor can we in every instance recognise the inherent loveliness of what it enjoins. Sometimes, if not very frequently, it simply commands us to submit, and offers nothing either to captivate the affections or charm the imagination. It is in this condition that conscience most nearly resembles a law extraneous to the mind, furnishing merely a rule of conduct and demanding obedience, but indicating nothing in regard to the spiritual condition of the mind itself; and it is in this its most abstract form that I would at present consider it.

What, then, is the first result of our knowledge of a moral law? In the language of the Apostle, sin revives. Sin is a transgression of the law; therefore the consciousness of sin enters the mind for the first time when it learns to distinguish between right and wrong. Prior to this period, uncontrolled desire brought with it no sense of rebellion against a legitimate authority. The appetites and affections went freely in quest of their several objects, and felt no shame, no desire of concealment, in their act. Whatever was attractive to the eye or pleasant to the palate was eagerly appropriated, without any uncomfortable suspicion that we were unjust or greedy. We defended ourselves from assault or avenged our injuries by violence, and never dreamed that the Spirit of Meekness could weep at our conduct. The cannibal dines complacently on a wellfed captive, and, far from feeling compunction, rejoices in his strength and cunning. The votary of superstition dyes his altar with human blood, and his heart never faints with sickening horror at the scene. David shared his affection among a number of wives, and his domestic peace was not disturbed by any thought that he was violating a sacred relation. The Israelites massacred their enemies, butchering women and children in cold blood, but never lamented that they had transgressed the commands of Mercy. But the case is widely different when Conscience issues her orders. Then men no longer appear with unabashed look, but hide themselves from the voice of the Lord, and go out with fallen countenance from his presence. Then they become conscious of the evil of untamed passion, and tremble before the calm, awful eyes of Justice, Pity, and Love. They feel that they are sinful, that sin has come to life, and lies like a wild beast at their door, ready to spring upon them. The stain of blood is a crimson spot upon the hand, that will not be wiped out. Pampered appetite is accompanied by a clinging sense of degradation, which, invisible but felt, goes wherever we go, standing behind us when brilliant lights and merry companions strive to exorcise such

a ghost, lying down heavily with us at night, pursuing our rapid steps in the morning, and refusing to
depart except through prayer and fasting. Selfishness
loses the highest pleasure of fruition ; sweet becomes
bitter in its mouth ; possession has not the charmed
aspect which it wore in the distance ; the violated
law, 'Thou shalt love thy neighbour as thyself,'
discomposes all our expectations of happiness. Thus
sin becomes a disturbing element in human life.
Wherever the light of the moral law penetrates,
actions assume a new appearance, and the joyous
face of innocence begins to wear the earnest look
of responsibility, the sadness of inevitable slavery,
or, it may be, the defiance of wilful rebellion. The
peace of Paradise is gone, and sin has come to life.

Is it said that this language is too strong, that it
is not sin which comes to life, but only the consciousness of sin, that men offended just as much
before the law came, and that its sole office was to
point out to them the evil in which they were already
living ? I reply, that the moral law does much more
than this, that it alters the very nature of the acts
against which it is directed, and furnishes the occasion
on which their worst features become attached to
them. Men may, indeed, in a certain sense, sin before
the commandment comes ; that is, they may commit
actions which are rightly described as sinful. 'But
sin is not *imputed* when there is no law,' and that
man is blessed to whom the Lord imputeth not

iniquity. In other words, the action which, regarded
in the abstract, we should pronounce sinful, cannot
be justly reckoned such when it is not performed in
opposition to better knowledge. And it is this
added feature of intentional opposition to a known
rule which imparts to sin its most pernicious qualities.
The mere outward consequences of an action may
remain unchanged, but the effect which it produces
on the character is totally altered. The actions,
however coarse and brutal, which a man may perform while ignorant of their evil nature, will not
harden and deprave him in the same manner as much
more refined conduct, which stands in deliberate
opposition to the authority of conscience. Unrestrained appetite, resulting from ignorance, will kill
the body; but only when it is mingled with the
sense of guilt will it slay the soul. No one will
maintain that gluttony is the same thing in a sea-gull
as in a man—in a savage as in a Christian. The ban-
quet of human flesh enjoyed in the light of day, and
without fear of reproach, does not taint the mind of
the barbarian in the same way as it would affect ours,
making us the vilest of our race, if with darkened
room, the door locked against any possible intrusion,
trembling lest the very walls should repeat the
horrid tale, we plunged our teeth into such an im-
pious repast. The barbarian would be as contented
and as ready for wise instruction after as before
the meal. We should be lashed with the furies of

remorse, and branded with a mark blacker than that of
Cain. We should despair of ourselves, and be hard
enough for any crime to which passion might urge
or interest entice us. Or, to take a less extreme
example, we may, in perfect thoughtlessness, ill treat
the lower animals. Children, without ever imagin-
ing that they are injuring the rights of other creatures, will pull the wings off flies, or ascertain
experimentally on how many legs it is possible for a
spider to walk, and pry in a manner painful to their
victims into other mysteries of animal life. Such
practices ought to be carefully checked, for the sake
of the little sufferers, if not for the benefit of the
children themselves; and this infantine pursuit of
science ought not to be allowed to grow into a habit.
But it would be absurd to say that this unwitting
infliction of pain tends to make the character fierce
and cruel. That result will follow only when Pity
steps in with her mild laws, and in opposition to our
better knowledge we persist in our wanton pastime.
If a man stubbornly withstand the pleadings of compassion within his breast, and, simply to gratify a low
taste, outrage an admitted law, then ferocity will sink
into his character, and from taking pleasure in the
torments of rats and cocks he will become indifferent
to the claims of human sorrow, possibly at last violent
and criminal in his conduct to his fellow-men. Or,
again, we may see the same truth illustrated by
comparing the observed effects of evil institutions

with those which, arguing from our own conscience,
we should expect to follow. In reasoning on such
matters, we are apt to leave out this important consideration, whether the guilt of the evil institution is
clearly recognised in the country where it exists.
If it be not so recognised, the deplorable consequences on which we reckoned will fall far short
of our calculations. If a slaveholder, for instance,
has grown up in the midst of slavery, if the public
conscience of the community in which he lives has
not yet condemned it, and if all the arguments he
has heard upon the subject have been in favour of
that system, then he may be something quite different from the ferocious monster which we feel
certain that a man would become who here, in
opposition to the laws of his country and the clearly
expressed conscience of the people, should attempt
to hold any fellow-creature in abject bondage to his
arbitrary will. This may account for the fact, so
incredible to those who cannot place themselves in
the position of another, that many slaveholders have
been kind and humane men. But let the national
conscience once come into violent collision with the
system, and then, if it be still maintained from mere
selfish greed, its foul results will develop themselves
in a rank and pernicious crop.

These examples may enable us to understand
how true it is that, when the commandment comes,
sin revives. It is a period fraught with danger

both to individuals and nations. When conscience is awakened to the evil of any course of conduct, it does not immediately gain the victory. There is in human nature a dislike of obeying a command. Restraint cannot be pleasant, and we may think we show our independence or manliness best by violating the law. The command not to covet works in us all manner of covetousness. Then old habits will not disappear without a struggle. They will question for a time the authority of the new law; and when that can be no longer questioned, they may, perhaps, rebel. Habits which were mere thoughtless instincts, and left hardly a trace upon the real character, now become determined passions, and place men in opposition to the Will of God. They were but accidents of the body; now they eat into the soul. They prevented not devotion from breathing its prayer, or singing its psalm of thanksgiving; but now they stand darkly before the spirit, and forbid the hands to rise towards Heaven. Or if there be not direct rebellion, yet it is difficult to overcome an ancient habit. After many efforts, we may despair of success, and believe that we are doomed to live in hopeless alienation from the Law. Despair may produce recklessness, and from constantly disobeying in one point we may proceed to disobey in many. Thus the entrance of light may be the commencement of terrible darkness, and the Law, which was designed to lead us from evil, may supply the occasion when sin takes its firmest hold upon the soul.

What wonder that our hearts should die within us when the severe purity of the moral law reveals itself in the conscience, and sin, aroused to life, appears to lurk in almost everything we do! Before it comes, we think it is to be desired to make us wise; and lo! when it has arrived, instead of our being like God, we know for the first time that we are remote from God. We are hemmed in by restraints on every side, and tremble at the very breeze, which seems to murmur our condemnation in the rustling leaves. Wherever we turn, some broken command meets us. Whenever our hearts would gush with native glee, we shrink under the stern question, Is it lawful? When we would start off in pursuit of pleasure, to bound with the antelope over the wild, to laugh with the merry stream, or read mysteries in the clear depths of the solemn sea, some duty interposes and frowns us back. Nature, which was all joyous, exulting in its robe of beauty, and sending up from its million creatures a blended hymn of praise, now looks sad; for we are out of harmony with its brighter aspects, and withered leaves and dripping rain seem more akin to our own mournful hearts. What have we to do with stars and suns, with carolling bird, or bee extracting sweets wherever it goes, with ocean's undying anthem, or the thunderstorm, grand in its resistless power? Can these read the secret of a burdened soul, or interpret the mystery of sin? Ah, no! From age to age they fulfil unconsciously the eternal law; but man, who knows that law— man born to be a prince over nature, and to be a mirror of the Great Spirit—disobeys, and alone bears in his oppressed bosom the sense of guilt.

Yet let us not close with despairing words. This sorrow of the soul is the price that we pay for our greatness. 'Through much tribulation we must enter into the kingdom of heaven.' We must be strengthened under the discipline of the Law, and learn the self-denial of duty, before we can attain to the glad and free service of love. God has greater things in store for his children. And though we must die under the crushing weight of responsibility and the attacks of sin, revived by the very Law which is meant to destroy it, yet we shall rise again clothed in the power of the Spirit, redeemed from the bondage of the Law, and fulfilling as free Sons of God his most holy Will.

XV.

THE SINFULNESS OF MAN'S NATURE.

ROMANS vii. 14--17.

'*For we know that the law is spiritual: but I am carnal, sold under sin. For that which I do I allow not: for what I would, that do I not; but what I hate, that do I. If then I do that which I would not, I consent unto the law that it is good. Now then it is no more I that do it, but sin that dwelleth in me.*'

THE first result of the communication to us of a moral law is, as I have attempted to show on another occasion, to introduce sin into our nature, or, more properly, to arouse sin into life and activity. Before the conscience attains to the perception of right and wrong, we enjoy a state of simple innocence, yielding with artless and irreproachable freedom to each passing impulse. But as soon as we become conscious of the law of right and wrong, innocence is henceforward impossible. We survey our nature in a new light, are made aware of its points of op-position to the Divine order; and if we persist in obeying an impulse formerly innocent, but now forbidden, our character is hardened, and we are

estranged from the favour of God. The sense of
violated law communicates to sin its most malignant
and destructive power, filling the soul with apprehension or despair, and imparting that feeling of
degradation which makes a man reckless and sinks
him ever lower in the gulf of mean desire and selfish
passion.

We might be disposed, then, to ask, Is not the law
in this case something radically bad? Should we
not be better without it? Why torment me with
a commandment, if the commandment only engenders
disobedience, and makes me vile in my own eyes?
If sin always appears concurrently with the moral
law, is not that law sin? If the dark shadow of
impending death and judgment falls upon the conscience the moment it perceives the rule of right
and wrong, is not that rule death, and to be dreaded
as the foe of mankind? We cannot accept this
conclusion; for the dictates of conscience are invariably accompanied by the impression of their
divinity. We do not feel merely that these are
commands which we should disobey at our peril, and
which possibly it might be brave and manly to defy,
regardless of the personal risk; but we feel that we
have no right to disobey them, that real bravery
and manliness can be found only on their side, and
to defy them and take the consequences is not
courage, but satanic obstinacy and self-will. Conscience speaks with the authority not of a usurper,

N

but of a rightful lord, and its precepts are the expression of a Divine and eternal order. At the very
moment when we rebel we secretly confess that we
ought not to do so, for what conscience says is good.
When we strike a resentful blow, or harbour ill-
will in our hearts, and conscience declares, ' That is
wrong,' however we may justify ourselves in words,
we inwardly admit that the verdict is true. When,
for the sake of our own low pleasures, we neglect
the calls of humanity, or through self-interest
outrage the requirements of justice and truth, and
conscience says, ' Thou shalt be merciful, thou shalt
not lie or deal unfairly,' whatever obligations we
may pretend ourselves under to expediency, the conviction will not leave us that the commandment is
' holy and just and good.' Thus the moral law
carries with it its own justification ; and whatever
evils may arise on occasion of its appearance, the
real source of such evils must be looked for else-
where. ' We know that the law is spiritual ; ' it
is man that is ' carnal, sold under sin.' All the
confusion that disfigures human life— the ferocity,
sensuality , and crime that distinguish the bad, the
errors and failings that so often sadden the good—
are not tacked on to us from without, but flow from
within, and are expressions of our nature. Out of
the *heart* come evil thoughts and evil deeds ; and
the operation of the moral law does but bring into
the light of consciousness, and thereby intensify

the discord already there. It is true that we sometimes speak of sin as a departure from nature, and
the most flagrant forms of it we characterise as
unnatural. Some moralists assure us that if we
only live naturally we shall live well. The truth
contained in such statements appears to be this—
that our nature, if perfectly healthy and harmonious,
according to the Divine ideal of it, would invariably
lead us right, and that our departures from the requirements of conscience are no less perversions of
the image of God, in which man was created. What
is this but to affirm that man's nature, as we actually
behold it, is something different from the Divine
conception of it, or, if we choose so to express it,
that it has fallen below what God designed it to be,
and is more or less diseased? Indeed, I know not
how any man can look for one hour at the world
around or into his own heart, and escape this conclusion. It is an obvious fact, that the world's doings
are not in perfect conformity with the Divine law.
What can be the cause of this, except that man's
desires do not accord with that law, but are ill-pro-
portioned and untrustworthy? In the brute creation
we observe no such contrariety. The beasts spontaneously fulfil the law of their being, and conform to their true nature. Man alone violates the
law of his being, and runs counter to the ideal of
his nature. And who can turn his eye into his own
soul, and not become bitterly conscious that the

relative force of his desires does not at all correspond
with their relative worth, but often the meanest
are the most prominent and clamorous, and those
which ought to be the glory of human nature make
but a faint and timid appeal. We see, then, that
the order revealed by the moral law is Divine and
spiritual, 'holy and just and good;' but the order
of man's natural impulses, though each designed to
fulfil a rightful function, is twisted from the Divine
ideal, and the Christian conscience in all ages has
mournfully confessed that man is 'carnal, sold under
sin.'

Perhaps this truth is never felt in all its clearness
and power till the will has embraced the side of the
Divine order, and striven earnestly to subjugate
nature to the law revealed in conscience. If we
deliberately set ourselves in opposition to that law,
we usually contrive to dim its light and partially
hide it from view, so that we escape the shock of
feeling ourselves utterly estranged from the eternal
Will. We practise tricks of sophistry upon ourselves, and muffle that voice of the inward witness
which yet speaks within us. Thus for a time we go
on our course with no clear consciousness of an
inward disorder, but with only a dull sense of un-
easiness, whose origin we are careful not to scrutinise.
And if, without such wilful opposition, we yet make
no effort to govern all our desires and impulses by
the rule of right, we shall fail to perceive in its true

light much that is wrong within.   Faults of temper,
stray thoughts which could find no admittance to a
holy mind, an overweening estimate of oneself, an
inordinate attachment to what concerns only this
world these we do not think of as distinct violations
of the Divine order, but, if we consider them at all,
we give them the gentle name of weaknesses.   It is
true, the word admits the very point for which I am
contending, but admits it with an apologetic air, as
if the case were really not so bad.   We shrink from
saying definitely and sharply, These things ought
not to be; they introduce a jar of discord between
my spirit and God's, and so long as they are in me I
cannot be truly his child.   It is only when we fix
our eye steadfastly on the spiritual rule, and resolve
to conform every affection, desire, and impulse to
its Divine requirements, that we become clearly
conscious how far removed is our nature as it is,
from that nature as it exists in the thought of God.
The most plaintive laments over human infirmity
and guilt break, not from the lowest, but from the
highest souls.   Not where conscience is defied and the
worst passions are permitted an unchecked course;
not where the sluggish mind is content with earthly
happiness, and never soars in aspiration to what is
infinite and imperishable; but where men delight in
the law of God, and would clothe their life in this
world with the beauty of holiness, do you catch the
sad strains of penitence and regret.   The noblest,

rather than the vilest spirits, will tell you how they have been tempted and bruised by the undue vehemence of their natural desires ; how Satan has often desired to have them, that he might sift them as wheat ; how their faith has languished under the obtrusiveness of sense, and their holiest longings have disappeared before the fierce inroads of passion. They will tell you how delusive it is to suppose that you have only to approve of the moral law, and then obsequious nature will at once submit to its leading. Peter knew full well that death was preferable to treacherous falsehood ; yet, in momentary terror, he denied his Master with a curse. And so others, who know and approve the good, fall miserably below their ideal, and pant in vain for a life of sinless grace and harmony. Often and often they do the evil which they would not, and leave undone the good that they would do. What breast so calm and holy as to know nothing of a besetting sin, and, while it glories in the moral grandeur of its nature, never to weep at its meanness and corruption? Oh, strange inconsistency within us !—now rising to the sanctities of Heaven, and adoring the eternal law inscribed with the finger of God in the conscience, superior to temptation, and conquerors of the world ; and now weak and pitiful, grovelling in subjection to things that ought to be our slaves, sickened with the tainting breath of foul desire, or driven helpless by the storms of animal impulse. Perhaps it is an excessive irritability which proves that we are not yet free. We know that this mars the symmetry of our lives, and hurries us into the use of improper words and deeds. We know that it interferes with that fairness and kindliness which others, and especially those nearest to us, have a right to expect. It disturbs our own serenity of conscience, and pierces us with many a keen regret. And yet, if we can attain to nothing above the law, nothing but the clear light of conscience and the energy of our own will, it seems impossible for us to endure provocation and opposition to our wishes with becoming calmness and sweetness. We are overpowered; and though we lift our heads with an air of freedom amongst our fellow-men, when we sit down at home, and draw aside our disguise, we shudder to see branded the word, 'slave.' Or is it avarice that eats into the soul? We see how paltry it makes others; and we vainly endeavour to conceal from ourselves that it is contracting our own hearts and making them hard and loveless. It renders us deaf to the pleadings of affection, and deadens all high aspirations and generous aims. Yet we cannot banish it by an edict of the will; but again and again its mean suggestions are triumphant. Or does ambition wield an undue influence? We endeavour to place it in its proper subordination, and yet we are nettled if we do not occupy the first place; and any fancied slight kindles our vexation, and perhaps our resent-

ment.   Or again, does some vice hold despotic sway
over us ?   We are acquainted with all its horrors.
We feel that it is degrading; we know that it is
undermining our health, and blighting our prospects
in life.   We see in the sad and worn faces of those
dear to us that we are making them miserable—
miserable those who ought to have their chief earthly
joy in us.   We are conscious that it is corroding
our whole character, creating fierceness and cunning
where kindliness and truth used to dwell.   We
know that the little ones whom God has committed
in solemn trust to our training are being corrupted
by our example, and robbed by our recklessness of
that wise and holy instruction to which children
have a right from their parents.   But injured and
weeping wife or husband, children defrauded of a
parent's care, and conscience, with its visions of
judgment and condemnation, all supplicate in vain.
The will is not adequate to the task.   We despise
ourselves.   We resolve.   We struggle.   But the
desire for lawless gratification forces its way into the
mind, till the whole brain is on fire with it, and every
nerve trembles for its guilty pleasure ; and, where-
ever we turn our eyes, we can see nothing that does
not suggest this tyrant passion.   Things holy and
profane alike are steeped in it.   We yield for the
sake of a temporary respite.   This shall be the last
time.   Triumphant vice laughs with the laugh of a
fiend ; and to-morrow we shall be weaker than to-

day. Oh, wretched men that we are! who shall de-
liver us from the body of this death? This extreme
case, we may think, concerns not us, though, alas!
it is fearfully more general than many of us are
willing to suppose. But, oh! is there any among
us who has ever looked up with eyes of worship
to the Divine and spiritual law, and earnestly desired
his whole nature to be governed by that law, who
has not experienced that sense of bondage which I
have attempted to describe? Who is there that
has never known a bosom sin, which has coiled like
a snake about his heart, and left its slimy track
upon the fair ideal which he had proposed for his
attainment? Will any say that he is absolutely
free, and that the reluctance or the perverseness of
his nature never holds him from a duty or turns him
aside to sin? If any thinks that he is absolutely
free, and has only to will the right and it is instantly
done, let him consider whether it is not mere
ignorance or stupidity that enables him to lay that
flattering unction to his soul. Let the Divine law,
in all its spotless sanctity, be revealed in his conscience, let his will rise to the task of self-conquest,
and he will then find that he is not higher than the
Apostles, but he too must 'groan, being burdened.'

But if we have indeed embraced the side of the
Divine order, and yet, through some constitutional
obliquity, do the evil which we will not, and leave
undone the good which we will, may we not say

with truth that it is no longer we that do it, but sin
that dwelleth in us? In its stricter sense, sin denotes
intentional violations of duty; but it is no false
instinct which has led men to extend the name to
that weakness of will and vehemence of the lower
propensities which gives rise to transgressions of the
law. This want of balance in our nature, which
prevents the will being truly Lord of the active life,
may well be described as sin dwelling in us. And,
accordingly, we speak of ourselves as sinful beings,
though at the time we may have no sense of guilt,
for guilt attaches only to the consenting will. But
is the subjection less awful because we may sometimes acquit ourselves of blame, and say, ' It is not I
that do it, but sin that dwelleth in me?' Is it a
pleasing thought that evil so insinuates itself through
our being as to deride our efforts and make life sometimes appear like a long scene of blighted aspiration
and withered hope? May we not shudder to think
that we are ever, in spite of our striving will and
repentant tears, the organs of a satanic power; and
that these temples of the Holy Spirit, so fearfully
and wonderfully made, are ever defiled with sordid
aims and gross desires, with fretfulness, impatience,
malice, distrust, repining? There are some who think
that this is man's highest state; and, if only wilful
sin be gone, we may take up our song of praise.
And is this our only peace, to be torn with civil
strife, to groan in captivity to a deadly foe, to

struggle with ineffectual effort to make our words the words of the Spirit, and our deeds worthy of Sons of God? Must we for ever delight in the law of God after the inward man, but see another law in our members warring against the law of our mind, and bringing us into captivity to the law of sin? Is the thought of peace a mocking delusion? Do we idly dream of a sweet and holy rest for the victorious saint? No; we shall yet thank God through Jesus Christ our Lord.

XVI

SPIRITUALITY.

ROMANS viii. 1.

' There is therefore now no condemnation to them which are in Christ Jesus, who walk not after the flesh, but after the Spirit.'

IN a former discourse I attempted to show that the relative force of our natural desires and impulses does not coincide with their relative worth, but that the contrariety is frequently so great as to induce in a mind which acknowledges the Divine order a sense of weakness and bondage. To conform by an effort of obedience all our words and actions to the severest moral law, while our nature, as it is, differs widely from the Divine ideal of it, appeared to be a task to which the will, generally speaking, is incompetent. Is there, then, no hope for man? Is he doomed to wage for ever a doubtful war, and strive in vain to do the good that he would, and leave undone the evil that he would avoid? If the view which has been taken of human nature be at all correct, the case would be so, if we stood in no other relation to God but that of subjects to a Legislator. If obedience is the highest term in man's nature, and, when we have attained to that, we have exhausted the capabilities of the human spirit, then, I fear, inward peace is but a delusive dream, and the dark consciousness of violated law must rest upon the soul with unvarying shade. For who perfectly fulfils the law? Who without presumption can rest his hope of Divine favour upon his own deserts? Who could stand without shame before the judgment-seat of God, if the voluntary conformity of his being to the Supreme Will were all that he could trust? But we have another relation to God, that of children to a Father, and it is the strength of faith with which we embrace this relation that accomplishes our deliverance. The state of mind which is induced by this faith we may briefly name Spirituality. We become conscious of a new and higher order of emotions and desires. Such expressions as faith, trust, love, adoration, living in the Spirit, communion, come home with a richness and fulness of significance which we never knew when obedience was our highest thought. Entering upon this state is a new birth of the soul, fraught with wonder and joy at its first entrance upon the visible scene. We might almost say that to the spirit it is a new creation of the universe, for nothing looks the same. God is everywhere. Each spot is holy; and in earth and sky appears a beauty such as only a

child of God can know. Then it is seen that it is
not so much nature that reveals God as God that
reveals nature, disclosing it to the eye of reverence
in all its deepest meaning and its rarest graces.

It is difficult to speak of this state of mind; for
to those who have had nothing corresponding to it in
their inner experience words must be vain and delusive, and it is easy for them to dismiss such ideas
as change of heart or new birth as the vapid dreams
of fanaticism. These may, indeed, like other holy
things, be liable to abuse; but to those to whom at
any period of their lives the nearness of their relation to God, and the conviction that his fatherly
Spirit mingles in the affairs of men, and lovingly
tends the individual soul, have come home in their
full power, the change which has swept over them
appears nothing less than a revolution, radically
altering their nature and forming an unexampled
crisis in their history. They cannot but speak that
they do know, and testify that they have seen, even
though none should receive their witness. Let us,
then, endeavour to approach this subject somewhat
more nearly, and consider in as simple words as we
can some of the particulars in which Spirituality
distinguishes us from the mere subjects of a Law.

First, we have here inward power, as contrasted
with an outward rule. Whereas the law gives us
nothing more than a clear knowledge of moral distinctions, and leaves to the will the whole burden of

directing the conduct in conformity with the requirements of right, spirituality implants goodness in the
heart, so that righteous actions tend ever more and
more to become the natural and spontaneous expression of the vital force within. The law cannot
quicken, but only guide; it leads the way, but gives
us no strength to follow. Spirituality fills the soul
with a new energy, and makes the rough places
plain for the redeemed of the Lord to go over. It
is a regeneration, a baptism of the old and earthly
man in heavenly affections and desires. The whole
nature is bathed in the purifying flood, and selfish
passion owns the subduing spell. Unlawful desires,
that had burned so fiercely, lose their interest. The
soul is full of God. The thoughts fly to him. The
heart cannot forget him.

This resting in God as a friend ever near, the
great author of life, the source of truth and goodness, is the distinctive feature of spirituality. While
we are content with a law of duty, God may seem
far away from the soul, his Spirit never mingling
with its deepest life or heeding its aspiration and
its conflict. No communion, therefore, is sought
with him, no prayer bursts from the struggling
heart, no superhuman strength arises from conscious
weakness and despair of self, no thanksgiving is
murmured for hourly blessings felt within. But as
soon as we know that God is our Father, our truest
life is perpetually renewed in communion with him.

Prayer ceases to be a form; the rapt soul catches the tones of his love, and in surrendering all to him finds itself unspeakably blessed. Not only where solemn crowds are kneeling, or where the silent hour is passed in private devotion, but everywhere is a sanctuary for prayer. Every pursuit is consecrated by it. No words, indeed, are used. No fellow-mortal knows how full the thoughts are of God. Worship is offered in the stillness of the heart, while the hands are active and the brain tasks its powers. Our love to him blends with every object of interest. We care for nothing in which we may not seek his sympathy and approval. The innocent pleasures of ourselves or others are delightful, because they show his goodness. Sorrow is mixed with sweetness, for it brings us nearer to his sympathy and consolation. The trials and disappointments in striving after perfection no longer mortify; for they cause us to feel more sincerely our need of him, and, in making us humbler, make us more truly his. This, I believe, is the 'faith' of the Apostle Paul, what he speaks of as the 'faith of Christ,' a resting as a child in God, having no will but his.

In this loving abnegation of self we find the power of spirituality. The law is constantly jarring against self, requiring us to act in opposition to inward impulses. But when we become spiritual, behold! self is crucified, and the higher Will acts freely in us.

Under the law our language was, 'This is right and we must do it, though it convulse our nature to the centre.' But now we say, 'Father, it is thy Will, and that Will is ever blessed;' and, instead of convulsion, there is peace that passeth understanding. Is our fault an excessive irritability of temper? We have seen that the law is unavailing. Not so spirituality. For though our sin may take that special form owing to our nervous constitution, and though fatigue or illness may aggravate its manifestations, still there is a moral element as well. It is opposition to our will or contempt of our wishes that excites our anger. Let the will be perfectly surrendered, let us be clothed with that humility which all must wear who feel the nearness of God, and the exciting cause is gone. Opposition to his will signifies nothing to him to whom the Will of God is everything. To be despised is a small matter to him to whom God's approval is more than the acclamations of millions. We may, indeed, be often grieved; for many act in opposition to God's Will; and the sins of others will fill us with sorrow in proportion to our love, and sometimes, perhaps, with indignation. But who ever lowers his own dignity or outrages the moral law in this kind of holy displeasure? It is only when a personal element is present that the too delicate nerves betray us into passion; and he who is spiritual has crucified that personal element, and sees things, as it were, with the eye of God. So, too, is it with other impulses and desires that lead us into sin, unless, indeed, we except those which, through long habit, have become a bodily disease. But even in such cases spirituality gives power to endure patiently the bodily distress, and to accept it meekly as the due penalty of former guilt. And owing to the new thoughts, affections, and occupations which it brings, it tends to diminish the force of temptation by driving it from its seat in the mind, and thence, by a beneficent law, to cure also the physical malady, and obtain at last 'the redemption of the body.' Thus spirituality cuts away sin by the roots, and expels it from its seat in human nature. It vanquishes that selfish element which is the source of corruption, and opens the soul to receive the full inpouring of the Divine Spirit.

Thus the spiritual man represents the true ideal of humanity. His nature is restored to harmony; and, if I may so say, the formative thought of God, no longer opposed by the reluctant will, freely exercises its power, and fashions him into the heavenly image. His lower desires are no longer fierce and clamorous, but perform their rightful office with meekness and reverence; and the higher affections exert unopposed their beneficent rule. The strife which never ceased while he was only the subject of a law is at last over. He is no longer torn by an inward war, nor sighs his hopeless aspirations while passion glows upon the fretful nerve. The force and the worth of his desires coincide, and the jar of discord is still. He is what God designed him to be, and the Father of all 'works in him both to will and to do of his good pleasure.'

We see, then, that our deliverance is not in ourselves, but in God. Our reliance is transferred from the strength of our own wills to his omnipotence. We have confessed our weakness, and owned that 'it is not of him that willeth, but of God that showeth mercy.' We have felt that, cut off from communion with him, we are but the poor victims of prejudice and passion—most so when we are most confident in our wisdom and power; but that in loving subjection to him we hear his eternal Word, and are supported by the might of his arm. Our boasting, then, is gone. We cannot say that we have kept all that was commanded us, and have earned our reward; but we are humbled to the dust by the poverty of our own deserts and the depth of the riches of his love. Sin has its wages, and earns death. But eternal life none can pretend to have earned; it is the gift of God, the free offering of a goodness that surpasses the thought of man. If we would glory, we must glory in the Lord; for his are our high thoughts, our holy feelings, and all that makes life great, noble, and free; and so far as we have any true righteousness, it is in His righteousness that we are clothed. How strangely different this trust, this self-abandonment, this joy and triumph of the saint from the weary straining and the baffled hope of him who knows nothing higher than obedience, and feels that obedience must ever be imperfect! Good would it be for men if, remembering that life is something more than toil and struggle, they would snatch an hour from their labours and seek in the stillness of their souls that voice which only the humble can hear, that strength which only the meek can obtain. Then they would see their path clearly, and truth and goodness would advance with tenfold power. A word spoken out of the hidden shrine of the soul is worth volumes of human wisdom; a deed inspired by the awful Presence which, known or unknown, is in every man, accomplishes more than days of our lower and self-dependent work. And have we indeed this wisdom so close to us, 'in our mouth and in our heart?' Is there a strength within which is made perfect in our weakness? Oh, be silent that we may hear; be still that we may feel! To be loved by God, to love him, to be bound to him in that communion which love only knows! Yes, this is eternal life, joy, peace, blessedness.

It may be said that in these remarks I have sketched the lineaments, not only of the spiritual man, but of the perfect saint. Are we thus, in an instant, snatched to our glorification, like Elijah in his fiery car? No; we must admit that spiritual life, as all other life, involves a process of growth;

and often, where yet it is prized and cherished, it
may be weak and sickly. But not the less true is
it that here lies the hope of our race, and our redemption is to be sought, not in voluntary obedience
to the law, but in loving submission to, and communion with, God. St. Paul, though he had received
the 'spirit of adoption,' counted not himself to have
attained. He felt that the whole creation waited for
' the manifestation of the Sons of God,' and even those
who cried, ' Abba, Father,' who had received the first-
fruits of the Spirit, groaned within themselves, waiting for the adoption. And so, with us spirituality
may be a very present power, the words 'salvation'
and ' redemption' may be but feeble figures of speech
to symbolise the Divine reality of which we are
conscious within, and we may seek our perfection,
not in mere efforts of the will, but in a faith in God
which shall convert us into temples of his Spirit,
and yet we may have many a frailty, to guard us
against any possible return of our pride. The excellency of the glory must be of God, and not of
man; and till our humility be complete, it is needful
that we should have many a fall. The spiritual life
must be ever renewed at its primal fount. As
soon as we think that we are sufficient to ourselves,
we lapse into sin. We attend to the bodily life
with unvarying care; but who seeks with equal
constancy the things that are above? We starve
the soul, and wonder that it is not in health. Thus

with most of us spirituality is fluctuating, now coming in full flood, and again leaving us dry and barren. We need an abiding love, a faith which through all vicissitudes remains unmoved. But the spiritual life requires fostering; and those who care not for the gift of God, or wilfully neglect it, must not be surprised at their own emptiness. Of the means by which this love may be fostered, I cannot now speak. At present, let us fix in our minds this truth, that to dwell in God and have him dwelling in us, to own no will but his, and to have that communion with him which springs from mutual love, this is the pathway to eternal life; and he who thus abides in God fulfils the righteousness of the law, and to him there is no condemnation. Oh, that God may touch our hearts and cause our deaf ears at last to hear his call, that we may turn in humility to him to whom alone belong the kingdom, the power, and the glory, and stray from him never more! Then we shall sing songs of praise, and our souls shall be triumphant in his joy.

NOTE.*

In the foregoing discourse I considered chiefly the last clause of the verse, and attempted to indicate the nature and power of spirituality. In order to give greater com-

---

* This note is offered merely as a fragment on a great subject. From a more elaborate treatment of it, I am precluded, both by the pressure of other labours and by the limits within which this work

pleteness to the subject, I must notice, however briefly, the relation between this frame of mind and Jesus Christ. The Apostle evidently esteems it the same thing to be 'in Christ Jesus' and to 'walk not after the flesh, but after the Spirit.' And indeed that high religious condition to which we gave the name of Spirituality can hardly be described by a more appropriate term than 'the Spirit of Christ.' He is the most perfect representative of that near communion with God, of that complete immersion of the self-will in the Divine pleasure, which is the main feature of spirituality. And, therefore, to be 'in him' is to be spiritually minded and to have access to the Father; for if a man have not his Spirit, he is none of his.

This may be less apparent now than when the first Christian teachers were proclaiming the reality of a communion between the Absolute and Eternal God and the frail and sinful mortal. The words were strange then, beyond the philosopher's thought, yet coming home to the ignorant and simple. We have grown up surrounded with Christian influences, and have been acquainted with men who possessed in some measure the Spirit of Christ, and represented in a form nearer to our individual life the faith and love which were in him. And we are accordingly sometimes less conscious that he is the originator in this world of true spiritual religion, that his is the one vast mind which gathered to a focus the partial and transient flashes of spiritual faith from earlier times, and set forth in all the fulness of its power, neither dwarfed by superstition

must be confined. I cannot, however, refrain from offering these few lines, lest it should seem that I made little of Christ's influence upon the soul. They may perhaps suggest more than they express; and the reader will remember that on many subjects it is easier to *feel* than to construct doctrines.

nor corrupted by speculation, that exalted life of the
Spirit towards which humanity must ever move or
perish.   But when St. Paul wrote, Christ was a solitary
figure, the one Soul in whom spirituality was to be
found, unless, indeed, we except the few on whom some
scattered sparks had fallen from that great Luminary,
and who all felt his immediate influence and acknowledged that his was the power that was in them.   The
Jew with his formalism, the heathen with his abominable
idolatries or his immoral scepticism, the philosopher
rising through the speculations of the intellect to the
thought of the Absolute, only to find that the Absolute
could hold no direct communion with man—these
are utterly unlike Christ in the simple majesty of his
worship of the Father, the stainless purity of his heart,
and the lowliness of his love to those who most needed a
friend.   His type of life is all his own, so high in
thought, so profound in devotion, so steadfast in faith,
so zealous in action and resigned in suffering, so full of
the light of another world and the voices of a heaven
not far off, that one often wonders if he would not feel
as much alone now as then, and wear upon his face the
same sad benignity.   It is not strange, then, that to the
Apostle Paul, living 'in Christ' and living 'in the
Spirit' were identical.   And if we regarded Christ in
no other light than as historically the representative
and originator of spiritual religion, and supposed that
the world, having reached its manhood, had no further
need of him, we ought, nevertheless, as a simple matter
of justice, always to associate his name with the great
principles of his religion, which may seem now to be
self-evident truths.

But more than this is contained, I think, in the words
of St. Paul.   Living in Christ implies far more of a
personal relation than has been yet alluded to.   Had he

been nothing more than an example outside the souls of
men, one whom they might look at and copy if they
would, his Spirit would have been only the Law reappear-
ing in another form. The intense light of his devotion,
instead of baptising others in the fire of the Holy Spirit,
would but have deepened the shadows of their self-
absorption. But he stood not aloof from the common
life of men, wrapped in his own sublime meditations,
and, in his intercourse with Heaven, forgetting the sordid
earth beneath. That sinless One shrunk not from the
saddest and the darkest scenes, but moved as a Man
amongst men, mingling with the sinful and the vile,
eating and drinking with publicans and sinners. Though
he was so far above other men, breathing, as it were, a
different atmosphere, and looking upon another world,
yet none was ever so near to them, so quick to read what
was passing in the soul, so intimate with every homely
sorrow. In the strong language of St. Paul, he was
'made sin for us,' bearing, through that strange
sympathy which only the Christlike know, the shame
and grief which ought to have been felt by others. It
was this love that subdued men and made Christ more
than the example and teacher, the Redeemer of mankind.
For when the compact of love is established between his
soul and the souls of men, they become conscious of the
subtle influences which pass from spirit to spirit, and a
new life rises in them, even the life of him whom they
love.

Hence, too, comes their faith in the nearness of their
Father. For what could that Spirit be which has so
entranced them but what he who sought not his own
honour always said it was, the Spirit of the Father
dwelling in him, and telling him what he should do, and
what he should speak? The glory of God, then, was
reflected in the face of Christ, and in knowing him we

know the Father. The chain of love has been let down from heaven to earth. God has ceased to be thought of as a philosopher's abstraction, the absolute and inconceivable, the unknown, of whom you can assert nothing more than that He is; and has become known as a Father near—oh, how near!—to his children, ready to fill with love, joy, peace, every soul that will submit itself to Him. Thus Jesus is not a cold pattern of excellence, but a Saviour dear to the hearts of men, one who sheds a new glory upon life, and baptises men in his own Spirit, and causes the lips of babes to praise Him whose name is ineffable, and whom the wise and prudent sought in vain to know.

XVII.

ELECTION.

A SERMON FOR CHRISTMAS-DAY.

JOHN xv. 16 (part of).

'*Ye have not chosen me, but I have chosen you.*'

THESE words, addressed to the Apostles, reminded them of the most important event in their religious history. They had not, after a patient investigation, chosen Jesus to be their Christ, and so conferred honour upon him by their adhesion to his cause; but, on the contrary, they had been suddenly called by him in the midst of their ordinary avocations, and, led away by the fascination of his presence, they had forsaken all and followed him. While they were attending to their nets, or sitting at the Custom-house, thinking probably of nothing less than of becoming fishers of men, or the exactors of a spiritual tribute for the universal King, they had been summoned to a nobler work—to share in the world's redemption. New feelings took possession of them; new gleams of truth mingled with their earthly hopes of a conquering Messiah. They had

not found the heavenly kingdom; it had found
them, and claimed them as its subjects. The same
process was exemplified even more strikingly in the
case of St. Paul. He was not an earnest and
humble inquirer after truth, but a vehement perse-
cutor, who believed everything opposed to his own
prejudices to be false, and all who had faith in a
suffering Christ to be the enemies of God. Yet in
the midst of his mad career a higher truth found
him, and chose him to be its servant. He was
struck down from his proud eminence, and learned
for the first time that he was blind, and needed One
to take him by the hand and lead him. He began
to discern that ' it is not of him that willeth, or of
him that runneth, but of God that showeth mercy.'
He had not chosen Christ, but Christ had chosen
him.

This choosing of the Apostles is but a pattern of
the method by which, through all ages, Christ gains
the adhesion of his true disciples. Christianity is
something above us, something which we cannot
understand till it has taken hold of us, and become
incorporated with our souls. If we look at it from
without, and examine it to see whether it is worthy
of our choice, we fail to perceive its finest features,
and our acute criticisms only betray our ignorance.
It is all-glorious within; and only the votaries in
its inner shrine are aware of its surpassing beauty.
Vainly we linger on the outside, and pride our-

selves on our sound judgment, superior to vulgar
prejudice, and seeing all the flaws in a system to
which men ignorantly succumb. We know really
nothing of it till one of its loving emissaries carries
us in, and fills us with the spirit of its worship; and
that instant our pride is gone, and we can only
adore.

This is the aspect of Christianity which is richest
in spiritual power. It is a message from God, a
call, a choosing of those to whom it addresses itself,
their election into a higher life. It originates
not with man, but with God: not in the human soul
painfully struggling upwards, but in the infinite
love of the Father coming down to plead with his
children. It is not man seeking for God, if haply
he may find him; but God revealing himself to
man, and filling his mind with unexpected light. It
is not a human aspiration after holiness, but a Spirit
descending into the heart with the power of sancti-
fication. It is not our righteousness unsealing the
fountains of Divine favour: it is an energy from on
High, stirring the waters of eternal life in us. This
is a view to which we naturally direct our attention
on this day, which reminds us of a great joy that
shall be to all people. We commemorate a *gift*
made by the Father of Mercies, in fulfilment of his
everlasting purposes of love. In Christ we have a
blessing which without him we had not possessed.
His Spirit, as we read it in the pages of his history,

is no creation of our own. Nor is it by our choice
that it constrains us, and subdues us in wonder and
love. We may, indeed, disown the gift and refuse
the natural authority of a Soul which is above us;
but that moment, though the outward aspect of the
gift necessarily remains the same, its spell is gone,
and our hearts sink back into their own coldness.
If it be true that we cannot know any man till we
love him, it is truest of the highest natures, and
only the disciple can understand the Christ. This
reverence, which, transcending the criticism that
concerns itself only with details, gazes with rapt
look at the whole manifestation and reads the
mystery of its inmost meaning, is not to be confounded with prejudice and bigotry. These have
always in them more or less of self-assertion; but
the reverence which simply abandons itself to the
inspiration of a higher soul is an escape from self,
and in this lowliness we know that we are exalted.
While we feel that in Christ God has chosen mankind for himself, and has not left us to the devices
and desires of our own hearts, but given us a Spirit
which is greater than our hearts and claims them
as its own, though our souls must sink down in
humiliation, yet then alone do they attain to the free
exercise of their powers, and in adoration of God's
unspeakable love discern that Light without which
none can walk aright.

This view may appear more clearly in contrast

with another view which has found numerous advocates. It has been maintained that Christianity is in
no peculiar sense a gift of God or a choosing of mankind by him, but rather the natural outgrowth of
human nature, a rising up of the soul to choose the
service of God. It was not a light breaking in
upon the darkness of the world, but simply human
thought glowing into greater distinctness. Christ, in
this view, is regarded, not in any sense as the ' Lord
from Heaven,' but only as the spirit of man assert-
ing its preeminence; not as the Divine Word, making
its tabernacle within the limitations of mortal life
and glorifying the natural man, but as the highest
expression of the natural, the type of what every
man may *make himself* by the normal exercise of his
powers. He thus becomes the revealer, not of
infinite love and condescension, but of man's greatness and independence. He is no longer ' a quickening Spirit,' whose awful voice disturbs the death-
dream of our souls, but the splendid example whom
we may follow, and possibly surpass, if we will. We
no longer sit at his feet, and revere him as a focus of
heavenly glory, through whose light we read what is
dark and mysterious in ourselves; but as containing
in our own powers the measure by which to judge
him, we tone down the impression which he has left
in history till he looks sufficiently commonplace, and
then we perhaps respect him for his faithfulness and
applaud him for his heroism and self-denial. We

feel no more ravished with delight when he says to us, 'Come, follow me,' nor tremble with joy when, after we have kissed his feet and bathed them in our tears, he turns and smiles upon us; it is well if we do not rebuke his presumption in claiming to lead us, express surprise at his venturing to pronounce us forgiven, and begin to instruct him in the duties of a prophet. He is not now the beloved Son, who speaks what he has heard with the Father, and who by the leading of his love would gather up all mankind into one spiritual fold; but one among many competing teachers, who expressed but a phase of human opinion, and whom, as chosen by ourselves, we may employ for our own purposes and at any moment dismiss.

These two mutually opposing views, which, at first sight, might seem to possess merely an historical interest, will be found, on closer observation, to concern themselves with our entire conception of religion. The question is simply this. In our religious life, is the initiative with men or with God? Is it we that bring down the Divine blessing, or God that lifts up our souls in worship? Is it our devotion that wins the favour of God, or do we love him because he first loved us?

In the one view, the highest doctrine can only assure us that, if we draw nigh to God, he will draw nigh to us; and if we reply, that we cannot draw nigh to him, there is no word of comfort left. But too often even this doctrine, which might at least faintly stir our aspiration, is denied, and we are confined inexorably within the circle of our own thoughts. All that we think is then robbed of its authority over us, and sinks to the level of mere opinion; for that which we produce must be less than ourselves, and our servant, not our ruler. Humility requires us not to be too confident, for we may be mistaken; and candour lowers our sublimest convictions to the same rank as the flitting fancies of men. In regard to goodness, too, we must work out our own salvation, and do it alone. We are not only to ' make our calling and election *sure*,' but to call and elect ourselves. If we choose to repent, and come to reconcile God, he will be appeased; but never will he come and cause the stony heart to gush with waters of life. Faith is the reward of our moral fidelity, not moral fidelity the result of an antecedent faith. Goodness, in short, is the meridian splendour of the human spirit, and not the dawning of the Divine.

In the other view, we are assured that God is near us, though we regard him not. He it is that lifts us into communion, and often causes unwilling lips to praise him. Who that has ever truly prayed knows not that his sincerest worship was no off-spring of his own choice, but rather came to him, and, without any volition on his part, snatched him aloft to the throne of God? When have we known the profoundest adoration of our Father's love? When have we most earnestly poured out our souls' desires? When have we felt the calmest peace within? Not surely at any moment when we chose thus to feel, but only when the Spirit chose us, and it pleased God that his glory should break in upon our darkness. Devotion is a gift, an angel of God sent to draw us gently from ourselves, and lead us to him without whom we can do nothing. We are not, then, confined within our own limits. There are things which are in us, but not of us. Truths dawn upon the soul which are greater than the soul, truths which we only insult by treating them as mere opinions of our own. We feel that they have authority over us, and have a right to claim our reverence and obedience. They are truths which choose us, and demand, not a careful investigation, but our devout submission to their power. It is no longer humility to decry them, or candour to place them on a par with our witty inventions. If we press them on the attention of others, it is not vainly as *our* thoughts, but earnestly, as truths which have mastered us, and which are greater than we. We are but their unworthy tabernacle, and can never adequately accept them in all their beauty and dignity. Let us, indeed, be modest about the form in which we present them; but let us not degrade them, and under the semblance of humility exalt ourselves by speaking of them as *our* thoughts. Rather let us devoutly say, 'How precious are *thy* thoughts unto us, O Lord; how great is the sum of them!' And in regard to goodness, do we never feel that God leads our reluctant steps, and that, when we have named our own spirits, we have not named all? Are we not temples of a Holy Spirit, that gives us monitions of right, and chooses us for the service of the only Good? Is not our goodness, then, only a surrender of self to him who has called us to eternal life, while sin is a rebellion against unbounded love? And does God indeed wait till we repent, and remain cold and distant till our tears begin to flow; or is there not a long-suffering which leads us to repentance, a mercy which subdues us and melts us into tears? Does he never reconcile mankind to himself? Does he never plead with them, 'Turn ye, turn ye, for why will ye die?' And as we advance in holiness, is the labour all our own? Are there no sweet and genial thoughts, no high and generous impulse, no meek-eyed trust, no faith in things unseen, which come to us as visitors from a higher world, and, if we will receive them, make their abode with us? Surely, if we know our own hearts at all, we have not chosen God, but he has chosen us. Lo! he stands at the door and knocks; let us open wide the gates of our souls that the King of Glory may come in!

The difference between these two views possesses

far more than a theoretic interest: it affects the whole tone of our religious life. The view presented in the text is, as I have said, the richest in spiritual power. The truth of this may have become apparent in the course of the previous remarks; but we may glance at one or two points in which it seems to have the greatest efficacy.

It is most favourable to awakening our gratitude. In the view which represents the first approaches to communion as invariably made by man, there seems to be hardly a legitimate place for this feeling, in regard, at least, to our spiritual progress. Our attention, in that case, naturally turns upon our own laborious efforts, which have only met with a well-merited success; and if we formally thank God that we are not unjust or covetous, we secretly take the chief credit to ourselves. But when we feel that God's love has not been won by our deserts, but, on the contrary, has preceded and been the ground of all our efforts, then our hearts tell us that we never can repay such love, and that our most costly sacrifice is but an unworthy attempt to respond to it as we ought. He loved us before the foundation of the world; he loved us through all our waywardness and sin. He chose us when we thought only of earth, with its toils and pleasures. He looks upon us, and asks for our love, when we deny him; and if in aught we dimly reflect his Spirit, it is by his grace that we are what we are.

To him is our gratitude ever due. Adore him,
O our hearts; and praise him for evermore!

Humility, too, obtains its surest refuge in this
view. So long as we think that we have chosen
God, that all our best thoughts and desires are our
own creation, and by our own conflict we have
achieved every victory, there is no place left for
humility. The wonder is, that we have done so
much, that we have borne ourselves so bravely, and,
though tied down by poor human nature, risen to
behold the mysteries of Heaven. We may boast,
and demand our reward, for we have acquitted ourselves like men, and our own power hath gotten us
all this wealth of soul. But when we remember
that the things of which we are so proud are not of
our own choosing, but are august ministers of God,
sent to bring us from the highways and hedges into
his glorious presence, then we are abashed, and
wonder that we are allowed to touch the hem of
his garment or to loose the latchet of his shoes.
And further, when we reflect that our grandest deeds
are but a feeble answer to his merciful call, while
all our sin is resistance to that Holy One who has
chosen us for himself, we can but hide our heads,
and confess ourselves less than nothing, and vanity.

And hence this view gives the greatest intensity
to the religious life; for never is religion so deep
and full as when, in utter self-abnegation, we leave
ourselves open to the unimpeded flow of the Divine

Spirit. This is the life of the saint, of the true child of God. He consciously lives by the Father, and his supreme aim is to be the organ of a Spirit higher than his own. If a man shut himself up in his own inclosure, and suppose that every advance he makes, every gift he lays upon the altar, is a meritorious service, he will perpetually revolve his little round of morals, and be a stranger to the kindling energy, the omnipotent strength of religion. But let him have faith that God has chosen him, that a higher Will than his own speaks within him, and that voices not of this world call him to glory, honour, and immortality, and instantly he will feel that he has a work to do, and how will he be straitened till it be accomplished! All obstacles must bow before the humble fervour of such a man. Life will cease to be dear to him, away from his appointed course. Visions of truth will come to him with greater clearness, revelations of the Lord in fuller flood. The higher his soul is lifted, the less will seem his past achievements; and forgetting the things that are behind, he will still press forward. The love of God will consume him. Its length, and breadth, and depth, and height will seem to surpass all knowledge. It will appear impossible ever adequately to return that love. He will not think that his labours can ever be sufficient to earn a reward; for what is all his goodness but the feeble trembling of his heart in answer to infinite compas-

sion? To offer body and soul to God is only to
accept his most precious gift; yea, to die for him is
only to admit eternal life. Oh, the depth of the
riches of his mercy! Brethren, may we this day
escape from all false and cold philosophy, and learn
once more the faith of the untainted heart, that
God's gift transcends the thought of man, that in
Christ he hath chosen us for Himself, and called us
to be his Sons! May we feel, in all the fulness of
its meaning, that 'of him, and through him, and to
him are all things;' and to him may be rendered
the praise and adoration of our souls for evermore!

XVIII.

THE MANIFESTATION OF THE SONS OF GOD.

Romans viii. 19.

' *The earnest expectation of the creature * waiteth for
the manifestation of the sons of God.*'

THAT a supreme Intelligence presides over the
universe is a conviction which has been gradually
expanding and deepening in the human mind. From
the time when every locality was supposed to have
its own special divinities, and the various forces of
nature were referred to the often antagonistic
wills of independent powers, how wonderfully has
the thought of God grown in purity and grandeur!
No longer regarded as a capricious and self-willed
Sovereign, he is now worshipped as the Holy One,
the eternal impersonation of the moral law, whose
will is coincident with absolute righteousness. The
woods and streams have parted with their patron
deities, only to find that he who dwells in them,
giving its verdure to the tree and its liquid crystal to
the brook, rules over all worlds, and claims the
immensity of creation for his temple. The farther

* Or, as the word might be rendered, ' Creation.'

nature is explored, the more conspicuous become
the marks of wisdom and goodness, flowing from one
central fountain through the whole empire of being.
The seemingly disjointed members of the universe
are being brought together; and science is gradually building up the various and once apparently
unrelated parts of our knowledge into a symmet-
rical whole. Fears are sometimes expressed that
science is injurious to religion, and that under its
cold processes the fire of faith begins to burn low;
and it may be that under the influence of a one-
sided intellectual activity, personal devotion has
lost something of its old intensity. But rightly
regarded, science is anything but injurious to religion, and is probably destined to be its great
emancipator, clearing away the obstructing prejudices of past ages, and opening the ears of men
to hear once more the voice of a Prophet, when the
fulness of time is again come. Its researches have
brought before our eyes a new heaven and a new
earth; and that sense of mystery which is the
mother of devotion is enhanced by the vast fields
of inquiry which it opens to the view. And it
deserves remark that those scientific men who seem
to feel least their need of personal communion with
God, and who would limit our knowledge to the
discoveries of sense, are by no means the least
impressed with the conviction that Law everywhere
prevails, and that the universe of being is a kosmos,

or world of order, in which all the parts are
mutually related and marvellously adapted to one
another.   Now, what at bottom is this conviction
but the unacknowledged certainty that, wherever
you go, you will find the great principles of intelligence observed, and that every particle of matter
bears in itself the marks of the same unerring
wisdom? If here and there we found the confusion
of anarchy, or if we discovered that different worlds
or differents parts of the same world were constructed on conflicting principles, and that the
natural forces could not possibly be arranged in any
system conducing to an orderly result, then indeed
we might begin to doubt whether, after all, Mind
were the ultimate, self-existent being. But when
the reverse of all this is the case; when science
forces upon the dullest and least spiritual mind the
conviction of universal order; when it has gathered
millions of worlds, as it were, into one dominion,
subject throughout to the same laws; and when its
tendency is to trace more and more subtle relations
among the various parts of the entire system, and
among the forces by which they are ruled, till we
feel ourselves members of an almost infinite community, and life's cares and troubles seem but a
ripple caused by a baby's breath upon the mighty
ocean—then we must admit how unworthy are the
fears that the prosecution of science should damage
our faith, or its amazing discoveries speak anything

but peace to our hearts. Had science set out with
a purely theological aim, to demonstrate from the
unity of the existing order of things the omni-
present wisdom and activity of one supreme Intelligence, it could hardly have achieved a greater
triumph for religion, or established more completely
the coincidence between the highest inspirations of
our faith and the results of observation and experi-
ment.

The view which is thus opened to us becomes even
more impressive when we not only look abroad
through the regions of space, and investigate existing relations, but look back also through vast periods
of time, and behold the gradual evolution of the
existing order of things. Our knowledge of this
subject may be still in a rudimentary condition ; but
sufficient has been discovered to impress upon the
mind the idea of one great plan unfolding itself
through almost immeasurable ages. Whether science
finally establishes the theory that the present complicated condition of the world is the result of a
slow, continuous development from the most elementary forms of being, or confirms the old opinion,
that there have been successive epochs in which, by
one stupendous act of creative power, an inferior has
given place to a higher stage of existence—the
religious impression will be substantially the same.
In the former case there may be less appeal to our
love of the marvellous, by which I mean simply that

which is strange to our experience; but the unity
of plan, the unwearying patience which, without
ever tiring of and suddenly destroying the old, is
yet continually working towards a higher and a
fairer—the ceaseless struggle, as it were, of nature
towards its ideal beauty and perfection—become even
more conspicuous. We learn more distinctly that
creative power does not burst forth at the end of
vast periods, and then retire into a self-imposed stillness, but is with us always, and day by day is
executing the purposes of infinite Intelligence, and
leading on the universe in the career of its wondrous
destiny. In the latter case there may seem to be less
continuity of plan; but we can still discern the
gradual unfolding of the Divine thought, and
perceive, in spite of the strongly marked stages of
being, a sameness of purpose, and a slow preparation
of the world for the reception of nobler inhabitants.
In either case, the fundamental idea which is suggested is the same—there is an order in the universe,
proceeding in fulfilment of one great spiritual purpose. 'The whole creation groaneth and travaileth in
pain together until now.' There is in it an 'earnest
expectation,' a waiting for some ideal type of being.
There is a raising of the dead and unorganised into
incipient life, of the living and organised into higher
organism and fuller life, of brute instinct into conscious intelligence, of blind conformity to a law
into moral surrender to the holy and true. Thus

science brings before us a series of facts answering to the high aspirations of our nature, and proving that there is a deep truth in our ideal imaginings and our spiritual thirst. However the tides of human affairs may seem to ebb and flow, yet the universe moves not backwards, but onwards ; life triumphs over death, beauty over deformity, truth over error, grace over sin. While the dumb rocks which entomb the relics of the past disclose their strange secrets, our faith bounds with a new joy ; for our hearts burning within us were warm with the fire of truth, and we may trust with a serener confidence the Word that speaks in our souls.

From the above considerations, it may appear that we cannot proceed far in the investigation of what might seem to be mere physical laws without being conducted to a higher order of inquiries, and having that portion of our nature touched which is too often supposed to be most remote from our reason. In spite of the protest of those who maintain that we can know nothing beyond the succession of sensible appearances, we are induced by those very appearances to enter upon a spiritual problem. Science reveals order, method, a continuous plan. What is this plan? Whither does creation tend? What is to be the finished product of this prolonged birth which we call development? Using a figure, may we not say that creation's earnest longing is 'for the manifestation of the Sons of God?' If we

judged only from our scientific knowledge, should
we not be justified in expecting that the final result
of the world's progress must be some high form of
spiritual being? The course of development has
been from the lower into the higher; and man,
incomparably the noblest of the present denizens of
earth, has never, so far as we are aware, had any
rival in the pre-eminence of his endowments.
Hitherto man has been the culminating glory of the
world; and if to him it owes its sin. it owes no less
its spiritual meaning and dignity. But man himself
is capable of development; and though we can very
imperfectly trace his course through the vast period
during which he appears to have lived, yet we can
see that he has slowly moved onwards towards his
ideal; and while individuals may have fallen and
nations decayed, nevertheless the race as a whole has
made substantial progress, and is nearer its perfection now than in ancient times. We can discern
no reason why this progress should cease, why man
should not become yet larger in intelligence, purer
in affection, clearer in conscience, stronger in will,
more fervent in spirit. Why should not the image
of the Creator be stamped more deeply into his
being, and the manifestation of men as the Sons of
God be the great goal of human society? To this
our faith and aspirations point. To become less
material, more spiritual, this is the law of our being.
The mind is our noblest part. The body is won-

derful, but wonderful chiefly as a temple of the
Spirit. Thought, feeling, faith—these constitute our
highest honour ; and to enlarge and purify these, to
bring the soul into a nearer conformity with the
Divine image, and make it more submissive to eternal
spiritual laws, ought, we feel, to command our most
earnest longing and endeavour. Towards this human
soicety must move ; and it will not be perfect till
every child of man is a child of God. This is the grand
consummation towards which, through incalculable
ages, our world has struggled on. And still the
struggle lasts ; 'creation groaneth and travaileth,'
oppressed with ignorance, sin, and unbelief, but still
fulfilling its law of gradual evolution into nobler life,
and in trust and hope 'waiting for the manifestation
of the Sons of God.'

These thoughts suggest to us a very important
class of inquiries, which, under the name of Social
Science, have recently attracted a large share of
attention. Admitting that there is a progress in the
affairs of men, that man's true position is to be a Son
of God, and that the great end of human society is to
bring man to this his true position, to endow him with
all intellectual, moral, and spiritual excellence, then
the question arises—Is human progress in any degree
dependent upon circumstances over which we may
exercise some control ? Do the characters of men
vary in some accordance with the nature of their
social arrangements ? Are there some institutions

and usages which are calculated to obstruct, and others to facilitate, the attainment of our true end? Such questions can admit of but one answer. However exalted a view we may take of the independence and power of the human will, however we may exhort men to be superior to circumstances and to force them into submission to their own high purposes, yet there can be no doubt that men may be placed at such a disadvantage, and be so crushed down under the weight of adverse influences, that only in the very rarest instances will they escape perversion, and rise above the moral disease and ruin with which from infancy they have been familiar. The possession of an intellectual and moral life may be rendered unnaturally difficult; the spring of cheerful health and animating hope may be taken away; the path to reform may be blocked up with insuperable obstacles, and those impulses which, in a normal condition, conduce to our highest welfare may be almost forced into channels of vice, and at last drown the soul in a sea of misery and degradation. It is well that all such circumstances, and the laws by which they act, should be thoroughly investigated, that statistics of the extent to which they prevail in our own population should be collected, and that measures should be devised for their suppression or diminution. It is well, too, that it should be considered by what means crimes against society may be most effectually prevented; how far a low state of health fosters depraved tastes and impairs the vigour of the intellect; what sanitary arrangements are required in dwellings and in work-shops, to improve the health, and therefore increase the energy and intelligence of our people; what is the result of unduly-prolonged hours of labour, and how may be combined the greatest efficiency in labour and the largest opportunity for happiness and self-improvement on the part of the labourer; what is the connection between ignorance and crime; and what plans should be adopted to secure a sound elementary education for every member of the community. These and all questions relating to human welfare and progress must possess an absorbing interest for all who love their kind, and pre-eminently for those who see for man a high spiritual destiny, who feel it almost with the pain of a personal rebuke whenever they behold a fellow-creature trained in ignorance and vice, who hear in the turmoil of life a groaning, an often unintelligent aspiration for something better, more satisfying to our soul's thirst, and who believe that at the end of all the tears and blood which stain the page of history, of all the guilt and misery and voluptuous selfishness which surround us now, will be the fulfilment of our highest hopes, of our most 'earnest expectation,' even 'the manifestation of the Sons of God.'

But we must not suppose that this great result can be accomplished by any mere social arrangements.

The most that these can do is to remove obstructions, or to afford facilities to the free play of higher laws. Our most skilful arrangements are in themselves but a dead mechanism, and cannot plant in the mind a single noble thought or generous emotion ; and we shall commit a fatal mistake if we begin to place our highest reliance upon these things, and suppose that they will exempt us from the necessity for personal exertion, for self-denying labour and sympathy and love. I fear that we are in some danger of this mistake at the present day. Opportunities are so abundant for delegating to others the good works which we wish to have done, provided they occasion no trouble to ourselves, that we have almost restricted the name of charity to that which is, in truth, its smallest and least significant act ; and having contributed of our money, we think that our duty is discharged. But man is not a mere negative being, to be driven hither and thither by the forces which are placed around him. He is a spiritual agent, himself the most mighty and the most original of all earthly forces; and it is his province to command rather than to yield, to direct rather than be moulded by institutions and social machinery. Unless you can infuse into his mind great ideas, a high moral purpose, and a strong and noble faith, you have done little for him ; and these can be communicated only by the personal contact of mind with mind, by the influence of the higher over the lower; and by that contagious power which is ever found in deep convictions, when pressed home with unpretending, heartfelt love. Let our social arrangements afford opportunities for this spiritual influence, let them bring us more freely into one another's presence, so that we may clasp hands of friendship, as children of the same Father ought, and show mutual sympathy and kindliness and desire to bless ; and then they will be fraught with great results, and help on that time for which all creation waits with earnest expectation. The mightiest power for social regeneration is and ever will be that of which the cross of Christ is the source and symbol. It is only the fire of his Spirit that can burn away the moral corruption which will bring a speedy decay upon the noblest institutions. It is only the quickening influence of a love like his that can kindle a new life within the soul. The most perfect scheme for the organisation of society, the most elaborately constructed associations for the improvement of the people, can only serve as vehicles for the transmission of mental power, and, if that power be absent, never can create it. One by one we must still take up our cross, and offer each some sacrifice of love, that we may add to the blessedness of others. A great, noble-hearted, self-denying man is the most potent agent for good that our brightest ingenuity has yet discovered; and it is only in proportion as we are great, noble-hearted, and self-denying that we can confer any true and lasting benefit upon our race. From soul to soul the subtle influence must pass, changing men from glory to glory into the image of the Beloved of the Highest, till at last the end of creation is attained, and heaven and earth rejoice together in 'the manifestation of the Sons of God.'

XIX.

THE LIGHTS AND SHADES OF FAITH.

Psalm xcvii. 2.

' *Clouds and darkness are round about him.*'

There is a problem which presses heavily upon the minds of many religious persons—How is it that God ever seems so far off, while our faith declares him to be so near? We believe that his presence enfolds us as an atmosphere; and yet, when we attempt in our reflective moments to apprehend that mysterious Presence, it appears to vanish, and eludes our most ingenious research. The devout heart feels that he is near, and asks no other witness than its own communion with his Spirit; but the heart is not always devout, and in our days of worldliness and indifference, when most we need him, his countenance is hidden from us. Faith in him we acknowledge as the very substance of our life, the only source of real nobleness and goodness; and yet how often does faith totter, and, without becoming a defined doubt with which we might grapple, lose all its vividness and power! At times his

authority rests upon the conscience with even an
awful weight; and again our debt to him becomes
shadowy and evanescent, and we cease to perceive
the Divine sanctity which separates right from wrong.
To make the majesty of his Presence felt in this
sinful world we own to be the only hope of its
regeneration; yet he never comes in the whirlwind
or the fire, and the sceptic's sneer incurs no miraculous rebuke.   Truly his ways are not as our ways:
and he denies to us the fulness of that Presence for
which we thirst.   *We* would make life one out-
pouring of reverent love, wherein is neither conflict nor fear; but it is often a hard battle with
doubt, indifference, and sin.   *We* would perpetuate
that unspeakable communion which is granted but
for an instant.   We would spend our years upon
the Mount of Transfiguration, gazing upon the
eternal sun, and conversing with the spirits of the
blest; but soon a cloud comes and overshadows us,
and a cross rises in its gloom.   We exclaim in our
impatience at human wickedness, 'Oh, that thou
wouldest rend the heavens, that thou wouldest come
down, that the mountains might flow down at thy
presence!' but all things move on in serene constancy,
and the quiet stars and firm-set hills are undisturbed
by the revellings of vice; and the awful eye which
rests upon the guilty heart never assumes a fiery
glow to appal the evil-doer.

There is danger lest this seeming inconsistency

between our faith and our experience, this painful
variableness in our feelings, should depress our religious energies, and cast a chill upon the earnestness
with which we seek the things that are above. The
prophecies of religion appear to be unfulfilled, and
the ideal glory which momentarily breaks upon us
from on high seems to mock us with an illusive light.
Those whose young fervour flung its own warm
colouring over life, to whom God and heaven
seemed nearer and more real than this world which
we see and touch, to whom religion was an over-
powering joy, uplifting the soul in holiest worship,
filling the heart with purest emotion, and almost
superseding the activity of the conscience and will,
may be terrified to find themselves, as it were, in a
lonely wilderness, compelled to combat single-handed
the powers of evil, and to say in the strength of their
own determination, ' Get thee behind me, Satan,' and
they may learn to question the reality of a communion so fitful and uncertain. One shrinks from
mentioning a difficulty of this kind, which so intimately concerns the soul's most private sanctuary ;
but I believe it is one which is deeply felt, and if
we can discover any considerations which may help
to reconcile this experience with our notions of a
fatherly Providence, they may be no slight aid to
our religious life.

The first question that presents itself, when we
commune with our own hearts upon this subject, is

a sad and serious one.   Is it any moral unfaithful-
ness that causes this fickleness of feeling?   Is it
God's countenance that is withdrawn, or is it our
souls that are hardened?   Are the clouds and darkness really round about Him, or are they only the fog
and gloom of our own sinfulness?   Can He be less
reliable in spiritual than in material things; and
while the light of day comes and goes with unalterable regularity, is it conceivable that the light
of the soul should arise and shine by no determin-
able law?   ' The pure in heart shall see God '—are
our hearts impure, and is our obedience the measure
of our spiritual vision?   There may be more reason
in these inquiries than we are willing to admit.
And though I do not believe they furnish an explanation of the whole case, it becomes us to examine
ourselves, to search diligently our own hearts, and
to seek that lowly simplicity and purity without
which assuredly there can be no permanent revelation of Divine things.   There may be no striking
moral fault, no faithless betrayal of our work;
but there may be a vanity and presumption, which
is no less fatal to the religious life; a secret
reference to self, which poisons the fountains of
devotion; an *obtrusive* love which seeks its own glory,
which is more akin to patronage than reverence,
and forgets the awful and unspeakable power and
holiness of the Divine Being.   And when this is
so, it is well that we should grope in the dark, and

dash our feet against the stones, till we learn our own insignificance, and return to him as little children, beseeching him to fulfil in us his own Will, and glorify not us, but himself in us. No man can seriously and humbly question his own heart, and fail to discover many a reason why the spiritual lamp burns so dim; and when we confine our attention to ourselves alone, the explanation I have suggested appears abundantly sufficient. Indeed, the reverent soul is amazed, not that the heavenly light is so infrequent, but that it is granted at all to creatures so unworthy; and every holy influence is received by it as a token of the most unwearying love. Once to *feel* the reality and nearness of God, to be lifted into a true communion with him, to be touched with the sanctity of unfeigned worship, infinitely transcends all our deserts; and the marvel becomes, not that clouds and darkness are round about the throne of God, but that streams of light so vivid ever and anon break through.

But though our humility may be content to accept this explanation, it is not exhaustive. The inquiry will return—Is it not strange that He in whom we live and move and have our being should be so impalpable that it is possible to forget him, and even to feel as if he were not? If what the Christian says be true, that he is our Father, loving every soul of man, why does he hide himself, why does an unbroken stillness reign in heaven, while

human passions rise and fall, while the trusting
prayer is breathed, or the coarse blasphemy is
muttered? True, we do not deserve the faintest ray
from his unfathomable light; but then, are not
those philosophers correct who scoff at the idea of
communion, who maintain that an infinite gulf
separates God and man, and that the latter must
therefore pursue his solitary track, and never meet
the Eternal Presence or feel his inspiration in the
soul? These are questions of absorbing interest;
and on a true solution of them depends the fate of
our humanity. Either we are to commit ourselves
to the guidance of positive philosophy, and seek in
science alone the direction of our conduct and our
faith, or we are to give heed to monitions of an
infinitely higher order, and to believe, although we
perceive him not, that a Father who loves us is continually beside us, and compasses our path and our
lying down, and that man has not only an eye to
discern the earth with microscopic precision, but
has a soul open towards the heavens to receive,
though it be in fitful gleams, the everlasting Light.

To me it seems that our faith ought not to be
shaken by the facts which I have mentioned,
whether felt in our own religious experience or
urged upon us by the scepticism of science; for on
no other principle could a field be provided for our
moral probation. Were the heavens visibly con-
vulsed whenever the arm was uplifted in sin, the

arm would be paralysed with terror, and the freedom
of the will be practically gone. Obedience would
be enforced by a constraining law. We should
have no opportunity of proving what we really were,
and should be unable to put forth our own interior
forces, and determine ourselves towards good or evil.
Righteous conduct resulting from an invariable com-
pulsion would forfeit every moral quality; and
courage and manly resolve could be displayed only
in the service of sin, for thus only would it be
possible to come into collision with our obvious
interest. Men would be the slaves of a higher
power, but never could be sons of God. The same
consequence would ensue if the existence of God
and his moral government were capable of scientific
demonstration, and we could trace the course of his
Providence with the same precision as the orbit of a
planet, or predict the period of his judgments with
the same nicety as an eclipse. No one thinks of
defying the laws of gravitation in the construction
of a house, or mingling an ascertained poison in his
food. The most abandoned criminal would wish his
walls to be perpendicular, and has perfect confidence
that a sufficient dose of strychnine would destroy
his life. And if religion possessed the same kind of
certainty as science, no one, except in obedience to
passions bordering on insanity, would think of violating its precepts. Far from its being an objection
to religion, that it cannot be chemically analysed or

mathematically proved, this is the very ground of
its existence; and if you could place its behests on
the same level as the axioms of geometry, you
would destroy its essence, and substitute a mechani-
cal conformity to a scientific law for moral surrender
to the Divine goodness.

The same remarks are applicable to the fluctua-
tions of religious feeling, and the tremblings of
a spiritual faith. For us the struggle would be
already over, the burden of obligation would be
not merely lightened, but absolutely removed, if
it were not possible for the heart to faint, and
for the soul in its agony to cry, 'Why hast thou
forsaken me?' In such a case, indeed, we might
be innocent and beautiful; but in no high sense
can we be holy till we voluntarily embrace the
good, and prove our allegiance on the arena of
temptation and doubt. The soft and meditative
qualities might be fully developed; but the manly
force, the self-determining power, the lordly majesty
of the soul, could never be called into exercise.
There would be no moral significance in our obedience to the Divine commands, but we should be
passive instruments of the higher law, and our saint-
liness would consist, not in the surrender, but in the
destruction of our own will. Were it not possible
to question the wisdom of our trials, where would
be the sublimity of trust? Could we not sink
under the feeling of loneliness and desertion, where

would be the triumph of faith? The entrance of doubt is essential to the very existence of moral freedom. Remove the clouds and darkness from the celestial throne, and man would be awed into submission, and the spiritual grandeur of life would have fled. But the blending of light and darkness, the vision of heavenly glory succeeded by the world's actual conflict, the descent of the Holy Spirit heralding the temptation in the desert, is precisely suited to an immortal being who is invited to live for God, but *allowed* to live for self. Were the veil never withdrawn, did a voice never speak to us from the cloud, were there no intimations in the spirit of higher things than eye hath seen or ear heard, we should grovel on the earth, and find our noble intellect and many inventions a curse and not a blessing. But, on the other hand, if the light were always here, and the obscurity of sense and reason never fell upon us, temptation would be gone, and self could put in no claim to our allegiance. The darkness comes to test the strength of our conviction and our love ; and thus God is seeking, not for the homage of those who are unable to distinguish his service from their own pleasure, but of those who will bear a cross at his bidding, nor heed the voice of the tempters, who declare that such is not his Will.

If we briefly examine the nature of faith, we shall find that it is agreeable to the view here presented.

Faith, it seems to me, is something quite different in kind from scientific knowledge, and is rather akin to a moral trust. This conviction is forced upon us by a very simple experience. We accord no admiration to a man because he believes in the rotundity of the earth, or employs a telegraph to transmit a message; but we cannot withhold our reverence from one who has an intense faith in God. We instinctively own him to be nearer the spiritual world than other men, and listen to his words as the utterance of one who is more in harmony with God than ourselves. This reverence would be wholly misplaced if his belief in God were merely a deduction, more or less probable, from intellectual data: and if his faith were stronger than the premisses seemed to warrant, instead of admiring him, we should deem him deficient in scientific judgment. Such, however, is not the case; and we cannot but feel that Channing is more reliable than Comte as an interpreter of divine things. The truth is, the world by wisdom knows not God. Seek him by the path of physics, and he eludes your quest. But he hath revealed himself to us by the Spirit; 'for the Spirit searcheth all things, yea, the deep things of God.' And while the intellect compels the visible universe to yield up her secrets, devotion is the only way of approach to the unseen and the holy.

This view is corroborated by the fact that faith cannot be transferred, like knowledge, from one mind to another. State a mathematical theorem, and make your demonstration clear, and your pupil will be no less certain of its truth than yourself. But try to convey your faith by a similar process, and though your reasoning may be approved, and your doctrine accepted, you will find the amount of faith unaltered. It will spread, like goodness, only by a moral contagion, by the power with which the spirit of one man appeals to that which is deepest in the spirit of another.

And again, when is our own faith highest and purest? When the intellect is most acute? When a chain of evidences is most clearly before our mind? Not at all. Our friend is already at a distance when we try to prove him still alive. And when our spirit communes with God, when neither doubt nor fear nor troubled thought is there, proofs are forgotten, and God himself is all in all.

Faith, then, is a spiritual quality. It implies the presence of high moral endowments ; and its fluctuating clearness is no more strange than the variations of our obedience and love. It is the light of life ; yet designed, not to dazzle, but to guide us ; and its lustre often fades that we may learn to fix our eye steadily and firmly upon the point whence it shines, and to keep our sight undimmed, lest we should cease to discern it, and grope in outer darkness. To question the reality of its revelations because they are not always vivid, or because on the minds of some they hardly dawn at all, is just as unreasonable as to question the validity of moral distinctions because some deny their obligations and we ourselves are not always faithful to our trust. And to deny the truth of spiritual insight because its visions are not susceptible of scientific proof, and God, immortality, holiness, and the communion of the Spirit are not included in the category of physics, is as if a blind man were to scoff at the existence of an object because it could not be heard, but only seen, and that confessedly only when the light was present and the eyes were open.

The view which is here proposed will help also to explain the fact that faith is clearest, though perhaps not always purest, in the early stages of the religious life. It is needful that Divine objects should then be presented with vividness and force, in order to awaken the slumbering conscience, and turn the heart with earnestness to God. The untrained will requires support; the warnings of the conscience have not yet shaped themselves into principles and convictions; and therefore a glowing fervour and unquestioning faith are given by Him who is best acquainted with our wants. But when the new life has acquired consistency and strength, and the soldier is already trained for the battle-field, he must go forth and prove his devotion in many a conflict with the powers of darkness. Yet, if he be faithful, the Light will never wholly forsake him. Calm and holy views of truth will take the place of the rapt vision of earlier days. Self-dependence

and trust in God will be harmoniously combined.
He will brace his energies to meet the onward host,
yet will not forget him in whom, though clouds
and darkness hide him from the view, is his only
real strength. And in the hour of bitterest trial,
the soul will rise up and assert its regal power, and
in prayer to Him who has once shined in the heart
will find the Light once more, and learn that its cross
stands out in such sharp and black relief on account
of the glory behind it.

And we may hope that when we have proved our
allegiance, and are brought into harmony with the
Divine Will, not by the overwhelming awe of his
majesty, but by free surrender to his pleading love,
we may then gaze on the unclouded light, and
mingle never more a strain of sadness in our worship.
What ages lie before us ere this ideal communion
with God be ours, it is not for man to say. Mystery,
bright but impenetrable, hides from us, like a shining
mist, a theme so vast. Only in reverence let us
wait; and however we rejoice in the visions of his
mercy, let us still trust that God will show us greater
things than these, and keep our devotion and wonder
ever young. Let us be faithful to every intimation
of his Will, and quench not his Spirit by our own
sordidness. If the light that is in us be darkness,
how great is that darkness! May He with whom is
no variableness, neither shadow of turning, keep our
feet from falling, and present us blameless before the

presence of his Glory! And if the meditations of
this day help to confirm any wavering heart, and
enable us to believe in the Light, and so become
children of the Light, though it be momentarily
hidden, thanks be unto Him who is near us when
we least confess it!

XX.

THE CHURCH OF CHRIST.

MATTHEW xii. 50.

'Whosoever shall do the will of my Father which is in heaven, the same is my brother, and sister, and mother.'

ONE of the means by which men have always sought to improve and strengthen their spiritual life is religious association. A desire for human sympathy in the highest relations of the soul may exist, indeed, in very various degrees. There are some who seem capable of pursuing their way alone, caring little for the encouragement or instruction of their fellow-men; while others crave the support of religious fellowship with almost a passionate longing. But the tendency which draws men together in social worship, and induces them to seek for spiritual help and sympathy from one another, is so general, that we may fairly treat it as belonging to human nature. For some minds the idea of a Church has a strange fascination; for almost all it has a significance of no small importance. A Church is one of the means by which we would escape from the narrowness of individual life. We feel as though there might be a community of saints, who, as a collective body, would present richer views of truth and purer manifestations of religion than can be found in men taken one by one. We feel as though such a Church might watch over her children with motherly care, winning all their trust and affection, and gradually drawing them up into the fulness of her own life. We would find there a wisdom farther-seeing and nearer Heaven than our own, in whose authority it would be well to confide, and from which we might accept as mysteries truths which only a riper spiritual experience could enable us to understand. We would hide ourselves in the manifold forms of her devotion, and, committing ourselves to her moulding influence, learn to love, to think, to labour, with an even and calm intensity. No longer driven by doubt and passion, ruled no more by the vanity of self-reliance, we would rest in the sacred peace of a spiritual home, waiting to be formed by its gentle sway, and permitting ourselves to be gathered at last into that perfect life which belongs only to the true, the ideal Church.

With such a longing implanted in their hearts, and an experience often so much opposed to their conception—thirsting for a Church mightier, holier, truer than themselves, and finding the spiritual life a solitary struggle against depression and doubt, engendered by the influence of others—it is not strange that men conceive the opinion that somewhere amid the rival pretensions of the sects there must be a true claim, that somewhere on earth there must be a visible Church of God, where alone the weary soul can obtain the waters of life.

The transition is easy from such an opinion to the belief that all except the one true Church are false and pernicious, and not merely imperfect patterns of the great ideal. Men have fiercely maintained that salvation was the exclusive prerogative of the Church to which they belonged, and that all dissentients from her teaching were on the high road to eternal perdition. And although this gloomy and horrible fancy is giving way to juster principles, and people are ceasing to believe that the everlasting destiny of a soul can be dependent on the anathema or the blessing of a hierarchy, still men's religious sympathies are not yet conformed to the Divine rule, but differences of Church association alienate them more or less from one another. The members of a dominant party may indeed condescend to admit that one outside their pale may finally experience the mercy of God; but they carefully exclude him from their own love, and scornfully repudiate the idea that such an one can be their brother. It is still, therefore, a question of the greatest importance by what principle we should govern our religious love;

whether any visible organisation does, or ever can,
embrace all the members of the true Church, or
whether that Church transcends all our artificial
plans, and is an indeterminate community, extending through all time and through all sects and
nations; and whether our craving for Church-
fellowship is to seek satisfaction in one of the little
sections which human zeal has contrived, or in the
invisible company of all faithful souls. It may
enable us to answer this question if we observe
Christ's principle of spiritual relationship.

The words of our text form one of those pregnant
sayings of Christ's, whose very simplicity seems to
conceal from us the depth of their meaning and the
extent of their application. We have here the
eternal ground of Church-fellowship, the one only
principle by which our religious love ought to be
governed. Christ did not ask where a man worshipped, or what form his intellectual conception of
God assumed, before he admitted him to a spiritual
relationship as strong as the dearest natural ties.
Fidelity to the Father's Will was his one test of
religious kinship. His own meat and drink, the
very substance of his own inner life, was to do the
Will of his Heavenly Father. This was the ideal
which kindled his childish enthusiasm—this the all-
conquering resolve which made his manhood the
highest manifestation of the Divine Spirit. And
wherever he found a similar religious consecration,
wherever he detected anything of the same yearning

devotion to the Supreme Will, there he recognised a brother, there he felt a bond of union which nothing could sever.

I know it is easy to escape the natural inference from this by saying, that the knowledge of God's Will has been entrusted to only one community, that there is only one authority which can proclaim this Will to the world, and that therefore submission to that authority is the very first act of obedience to God. This was the old argument against heretics, who, however pure and noble their lives, were supposed to be in a state of refractory disobedience, and never to have made the first needful act of submission. It is by such ingenious, though perhaps often undesigned sophistries, that men seek to transfer to themselves the homage which is due to God alone. I say sophistries; for is not such a limitation completely opposed to the clear meaning of Christ? He never gives the slightest hint of any such limitation. He never objects to the Pharisees that they were zealously endeavouring to do God's Will, but were mistaken as to its nature. His one objection to them is, that they are full of self-will, and while they pretend to worship God, they in reality worship themselves. And is it not evident that in principle he is disobedient to God's Will who is accidentally performing it, while he believes that he is opposing it; and that he, on the other hand, is a loyal servant who, while he humbly and faithfully endeavours to do the Will of God, yet fails through an error of judgment or the inevitable frailty of human nature? A lowly, earnest heart, which is simply bent on speaking that which it hears, and doing that which is ordered in the central shrine of its own conscience and faith, would surely come under the rule of Christ, and receive his glad welcome as a member of his Church. Such a principle seems grounded in justice, and it is hardly possible for us to dissent from it till our passions are aroused, and our proud self-will takes the place of that holy, peaceful, all-righteous Will, for whose honour we pretend to be so jealous. Those who shrink from their own selfishness, and adore the higher Will, are drawn to one another; and the variety of manifestation which that Will may assume will not drive them asunder, but simply deepen their humility. Self-seeking is the principle of separation, the cause of estrangement from God and from one another; but that love which seeketh not her own, but aspires only to know and to do the Father's Will, is the principle of unity, the ground of fellowship with the Father and the Son, and with all, therefore, who share that fellowship. Here, then, we have a test of the true Church, of the Church of Christ; it is a community of the faithful—of those who hear the Word of God, and do it.

Now, when we apply this criterion to determine the true Church, can we locate or define it? Can

we pretend that there is any association of men
which comprises within itself all the faithful, which
is the sole repository of all real goodness, and beyond
which there is nothing but rebellion and sin? Can
we say that love, resignation, trust, piety, worship in
spirit and in truth, earnest self-sacrificing devotion to
the Father's Will, are the exclusive possession of
any sect, or can be obtained only by submission to
some ecclesiastical authority? Few have the
hardihood to make an assertion so palpably false;
but men are continually thrusting these, which form
the very soul and substance of Christianity, into the
background, advancing exorbitant claims on behalf
of things of very minor importance, and regulating
their religious sympathies by erroneous tests. It is
readily conceded that the true Church, to whatever
sect for the time being that name may be applied,
includes many unworthy members, and that with its
genuine wheat tares are undistinguishably mixed;
but men shrink from admitting the obvious converse
of this fact, that among the tares beyond the little
inclosure true wheat is to be found, and that in every
corner of the world's great field the genuine and
the spurious harvests are growing side by side. This
doctrine, which is set forth by Christ with such a
clear emphasis in the Parable of the Tares, and in a
manner even more striking in that of the Good
Samaritan, is confirmed by his test of spiritual
relationship. Taking this as a clue, we may pass

through the sects and nations, and we shall find that the Church of his spiritual kindred is quite different from all existing associations, that it appears in varying proportions within the limits of all, and far transcends the boundaries of any single organisation. He who insisted that the Jew should love the Samaritan on account of his goodness would also insist that for the same quality we should love a Jew, a Mahommedan, or a deist; and he would show how we misinterpreted the great law of brotherly love and spiritual communion, unless our estimate of the value of goodness were so high, and our devotion to the Father's Will so intense, that wherever we observed the presence of these, in spite of all minor differences, our hearts would go forth to welcome them with fraternal sympathy and good will. Those whom he regarded as brothers and sisters we may not treat with coldness and scorn; and if we ever shut up our hearts against one who follows not with us, but has surrendered himself to God, although we may fancy we are doing honour to the name of Christ, we are but wounding his Spirit, and proving that we are not his. Those whom he loves we may not hate or despise; but our hearts too must roam over the world, and gather into their wide embrace, as brothers, sisters, and mothers, all who do the Will of our Father which is in heaven.

If this be so, must we not admit the bold paradox

that the Church of Christ is something quite different from the Christian Church? The Christian Church is a community of believers which took its origin from the life and teaching of Christ, an assemblage of men who consciously look to him as their spiritual teacher and Lord, and who with very varying clearness understand his doctrine, with very varying fidelity obey his precepts. But the Church of Christ is composed of those of all times and peoples who have surrendered their wills to the Divine, and have consciously turned towards God as the supreme object of their hearts' devotion. The scroll of righteous names in the Christian Church includes but a portion of those inscribed in the great book of the Church of Christ. Sameness of Spirit is with him the one bond of union; all, of every name, who share his Spirit are included in his Church.

Is it said that I lower the dignity of Christ by thus extending the true Church beyond the pale of his disciples, and claiming the possibility of fellowship with him for any who are not called by his name? I reply, that it is a strange way of maintaining the dignity of Christ to disown his principles and to violate his Spirit, and that the one only way of honouring him is to listen reverently to his teachings, and to imbibe the spirit of his life. If he said, ' Whosoever shall do the Will of my Father which is in heaven, the same is my brother, and sister, and mother,' it is not to honour, but to insult him, to insist on applying any other test; and we have not, with trust and love, sacrificed our own narrowness and our own earthly notions of greatness to the expansiveness of his heavenly Spirit, till our sympathies flow freely and unconstrainedly in accordance with this rule. We honour him by representing his as the one great Soul which rose up to embrace the principles of the Divine government, and which poured forth its love, not in conformity with ephemeral beliefs and worldly distinctions, but guided by the imperishable rules of justice, and the highest and only enduring law of spiritual affinity. We honour him too, we place him in a position of unrivalled pre-eminence, when we feel, as I feel with my whole heart, that under God he is the rightful Prince, not only of the Christian Church, but of the true, the Universal Church of God's faithful children, and that the possession of, or at least the thirst for, his Spirit is the sole test of genuine membership in that Church. How apt we are to honour him with outward titles and unmeaning eulogies, as though he cared for the gaudy trappings of an earthly kingdom; but how seldom do we honour him by an awe, a reverence, a silent, almost worshipping love, which leads us too to take up our cross, and become his brothers by doing the Will of our Father which is in heaven.

And now let us dwell for a moment on the grandeur of the conception at which we have arrived.

It may give a moment's pain to our earthly nature
to discover that there is no organised and visible
Church where we may hide ourselves, and find full
satisfaction for our highest sympathies—no section
of mankind to which we may entrust the keeping of
our spiritual life. We may feel an instant's loneliness when we step forth from the embrace of sect
or party, and become members of a great invisible
abstraction. But the pain, the loneliness, soon pass
away, and are succeeded by a sense of freedom, of
catholicity, of Divine sympathies and affections.
The Universal Church of the faithful ceases to be
an abstraction when the noble thoughts, the pure
devotion, the holy lives of its saints begin to fill
the soul. We then feel that time and space are no
barrier to spiritual communion, and that we have
entered into a very real Church, which began in the
infancy of time, which shall endure through eternity,
and which exists at this moment both on earth and
in heaven. It is true that any attempt to present
this Church to the eye as a complicated organism,
any endeavour to reduce this Kingdom of God to
the pattern of earthly monarchies, must end in
failure; and to the sensuous side of our nature it
must ever remain a cold and barren fancy. But to
the soul it is a grand reality, breaking the fetters of
time and place and party, enlarging the ideas and
sympathies, and raising us towards the perfect life
of humanity. Let it not be hinted that the dead

can have no power over us. Yea, they have the
greatest power; for the veil of time is fallen off,
and that only which was essential in them wins its
way to the mind. Their profound thoughts open
new depths in our souls; their burning words cause
the heart to beat with nobler desire; their self-
denying deeds touch the springs of our enthusiasm.
He who would follow the rule of Christ will
gather to himself the good, whether present or
departed, of every clime, of every sect, and cull
from each some rich lesson of wisdom or piety.
Thus only will he find that maternal Church for
which the spirit so often pines, a Church larger
than himself, 'filled with all the fulness of God.'
We must learn to see the pretensions of particular
Churches dissolve like the baseless fabric of a
dream; but the Universal Church of those who do
the Will of the Heavenly Father shall never pass
away: it is built on the Eternal Rock, and the gates
of hell shall not prevail against it.

My brethren, would we enter into this true
Church, would we escape from earth's mist and
strife into the upper air, and feel the power of the
invisible tie of God's Spirit, then we must accept
the one condition of membership: we must seek
with all humility, earnestness, and self-sacrifice to
do the Will of our God; we must feel that Will to be
all-blessed, all-holy; we must love it, revere it,
cherish it as the very substance of our hearts'

desire. Without this we may boast of our Church connection, we may be honoured for our zeal by our little sect, but we shall be excommunicated from the Church of the first-born, and the holiest Son of the Universal Father will disclaim having ever known us. But with it, we may be scorned by the world, and have our names cast out as evil by proud ecclesiastics, but we shall have our own sweet communion, the saints of all times shall fold us round, and he who sits on the right hand of Divine Power will stretch forth his arms towards us, saying, ' Behold my mother and my brethren!' Oh, this is the very bliss of Heaven, to love and to be loved by the holiest and best, and together with them to be received home to our Father, whom all true hearts adore, and in the peacefulness of whose Spirit we would worship with a voiceless praise!

XXI.

THE COMMUNION OF WORSHIP.

DEUTERONOMY viii. 3.

' Man doth not live by bread only, but by every word that proceedeth out of the mouth of the Lord doth man live.'

To any being utterly incapable of religion, our weekly gatherings for worship would present a singular and unintelligible spectacle. That men, one day in seven, should close their places of business, put a stop to nearly all the important work in society, assemble in crowds in buildings specially reserved for that purpose, and then not even confer with one another, but wrap themselves in silent thought, or repeat together exactly the same words, would seem to such an one the action of fools. What could they mean? What possible benefit could result from this kind of proceeding? What egregious waste of time! What inexplicable stupidity! Not having in himself the means of interpretation, our supposed observer would be unable to give a true account of the simplest religious rites. Spiritual things are spiritually discerned; and in order to change his view, you must let in upon his heart a flood of religious life. Then he will understand that 'man doth not live by bread only, but by every word that proceedeth out of the mouth of the Lord;' and the assembling of crowds hungering after words of God, desiring to bathe their soiled and weary souls in waters of life which flow from him, and to lose their narrowness of view and their selfishness of purpose in the consciousness of brotherhood and of a common filial relation to the Infinite Father, will appear the grandest and most impressive sight that our world can present.

Although we have been in the habit of joining in public worship all our lives, and may be presumed to know what we mean by this service, it may not be unprofitable to us to endeavour to clear our thoughts upon the subject, and to give a distinct answer to the questions—Why do we assemble ourselves for worship? and what conditions ought we to require in any one whom we admit to our worship?

First, then, worship has its ground in our natural constitution. It satisfies a spiritual want, just as truly as bread satisfies our hunger. We have been gifted with the power of looking up to infinite Wisdom and Goodness, and with a special class of feelings which arise in the contemplation of that which is above us. There is the feeling of solemnity and awe in the presence of the mysterious. Re-

verence bows before a higher goodness. Adoration
lifts its entranced gaze to immeasurable power,
controlled by omniscient wisdom. Aspiration glows
at the thought of kinship between us and the
eternal Spirit who called us into being. Penitence
weeps at the contrast between our attainments and
our capabilities. Filial love reposes with simple
trust on the forgiving love of the Father. To
refuse all expression to these feelings would be a
rude violation of our nature. The soul lives by
worship; and it is in obedience to a strong craving
implanted in the heart by God, that we bend ourselves in prayer before him.

But why, then, is not worship confined within the
secrecy of our own bosoms? Why does this most
modest and shrinking of all our sentiments, which
hardly dares utter itself before a familiar friend,
seek irrepressibly for public manifestation? This
is due to the desire for fellowship which attends
almost every human impulse. Literature, science,
commerce, philanthropy, all bring men together in
groups; and even the bodily necessity of eating
and drinking seeks to refine itself by social plea-
santry and the play of genial thought. Religion is
no exception to the rule. Our common participation in the feelings of worship demands for them a
common expression. It is as inevitable that men
should meet together as worshippers as that they
should form associations for the pursuit of knowledge,

or assemble in parties for interchanging the graces
of friendship. Without sympathy, the higher feelings would either languish or blaze into an ill-
regulated fervour; but when, in the congregation,
the same spirit of reverence folds us round, and
with united aspiration we surrender our hearts,
we are strengthened by this solemn testimony that
worship is the common heritage of the human soul,
and our feelings, insensibly exerting a mutual control, warm with a purer flame.

Besides participating in the general social tendency of human nature, there is a further reason why
worship should draw men together: it is itself the
deepest ground of human fellowship. Nothing so
powerfully binds soul to soul as the conscious acknowledgment of the same relation to the Heavenly
Father. Intellectual conferences may only separate
us from one another. The common pursuit of wealth
or fame, or even of truth, may fail to reach the more
hidden springs of friendship. But it is impossible
for men really to pray together, and send up one
mingled offering to the God and Father of them all,
and then rise without mutual affection and a holier
sense of brotherhood. Accordingly, in that form of
religion which we believe to be the purest, fellowship
with the Son is as integral a part as fellowship with
the Father. True worship, acknowledging that our
nature has its ground in God, recognises at once our
filial dependence upon infinite Love and our brotherly

communion as children of the same Father and heirs
of the same Spirit of sonship.   In proportion as our
worship is sincere, the offering of the soul to God in
spirit and in truth, we offer also our hearts to one
another, and experience that communion of the Holy
Spirit which every week we invoke, and the blessedness of which, I trust, we largely share.

It may be said, however, that I am here presenting
an imaginary picture; for in reality no sentiment has
so embittered men against one another as this very
sentiment of worship.   It has been the parent of the
most sanguinary persecutions; and when a more
genial civilisation admits men indiscriminately to the
same political privileges, and mingles them in the
friendly intercourse of trade, their worship is the one
thing that keeps them still asunder.   The idea that
the existing lines of demarcation may ever be broken
down, and that men may discover their real brotherhood by offering a common worship, is scorned as
Utopian by those practical men who, however
imperfectly they may read the signs of the times, feel
very correctly the pulse of the present passion; and
the doctrine that the State ought to show equal
favour to all religious sects is regarded by a large
part of the world of worshippers as the compromise
of earthly expediency, rather than a faint imitation
of the impartiality of God.   In spite of these
adverse appearances, I venture to think that it has
never been men's worship which has given rise to

mutual alienation. Rather has it been the decay of worship, and the consequent substitution of the form for the spirit. It has been the intrusion of self-love into the holiest sanctuary of the heart. It has been that disposition to exalt ourselves and our own peculiarities, which is the very antithesis of worship. As the spirit of exclusiveness comes in, the spirit of worship goes out: and as soon as we admit the cold, suspicious, supercilious feeling that others are not fit to worship with us, we have laid our own worship in the dust. Then we may try to heat our waning fervour with ritualistic splendours, and to consecrate our bitter zeal by calling it devotion to God; and men may speak of this as our worship, but worship it is not. I do not mean, however, to say that men's worship may not be most *sincere*, while much of the exclusive spirit still remains, but only that the *purest* worship results in the widest and deepest charity. Worship and bigotry are two antagonistic spirits, which may long coexist, appearing with rapid variation in the mind, but aiming always at mutual extermination. The thirst of the heart for purer wells of life, the bending of the soul before transcendent goodness, the fearful self-dedication of the will which knows too well its own fickleness, the sense of imperfection and sin and darkness which can obtain peace only by losing itself in God, the simplicity of aim which is ready to give up the dearest prejudices if the voice of God should so direct, the humility which is never mortified to find that it was wrong, but only grateful that it has been redeemed from its error—these are the feelings which enter into worship; and, far from dividing men, they are the very fountains of a large charity and of a tender brotherly sympathy. If we know that others thirst for the same perfection as ourselves, the feeling of communion will preponderate over every other, and it will matter comparatively little whether we drink the regenerating water from a silver or a crystal bowl, or, with untutored simplicity, from the pebbly mountain channel, under the free sky. Could we but kindle in men's hearts the real sentiments of worship, could we but turn all faces towards the central Glory, those on opposite sides would see the same holy light reflected from varying features and diverse costumes: they would gladly admit that to these also, as to themselves, God had given the Holy Spirit, and the circle of brotherhood would be complete.

Such thoughts as these are, I believe, slowly but surely making their way amongst men, and are destined to produce a greater revolution in England than was effected at the time of the Reformation. In spite of the scoff of unbelief, and the fury of ecclesiasticism, men are beginning to look calmly at their differences, to lose their human hatreds in the Divine love, and to feel that, wherever and however men worship, there is in their worship a common ground for mutual respect.

In the light of these thoughts, let us ask, What conditions ought we to require in any one whom we admit to the communion of worship? The evident answer seems to be, that we ought not to require any conditions, except that general sympathy in our worship which leads him to seek admission. This is the answer which has been practically given to the question by the old English Presbyterian congregations; but as the principle which it involves is, perhaps, not always consciously held, and as it is inconsistent with the practice which largely prevails, it may be advantageous to look it fairly in the face.

I think it will be admitted that worship is so important an interest in human nature, that singly it is entitled to a society for its common expression, and that even as a business arrangement it is not desirable, when you have formed a society for one purpose, to introduce a number of other purposes, especially if any of these can interfere with the main object. Now the object of a Christian congregation is common worship, communion with God as our Father, communion with one another as brethren before him; and if this worship is to have its largest and richest life, and to produce its most blessed fruits, it ought to rest upon the broadest possible basis. The more varied the tendencies of human development, the more divergent the forms of thought which it can succeed in bringing into fraternal union—the more noble, the more

impressive, and the more useful will be the worship.
The so-called worship which deifies a sectional
peculiarity, and draws tighter the already too-re-
stricted limits of our sympathy, only injures and de-
grades us. The real worship, which makes us feel
that we are numbered among the countless millions
of God's children, which raises us a step nearer to the
infinite life of God, and causes any word of his to
enter with its healing nourishment amid the diseases
of our passion and prejudice, redeems and sanctifies
our souls. And it is that this blessed result may
be secured, it is that worship may be clothed with
the undivided majesty of its power, that we refuse
to impose limiting conditions on our fellow-wor-
shippers, and are ready to welcome all who would
not live by bread alone, but by every word that
proceedeth out of the mouth of God.

To come to particulars, we impose no dogmatic
conditions. Neither ministers nor people have ever
subscribed a creed or vowed any theological allegiance except to truth alone. These venerable
walls * are dedicated to the worship of Almighty
God, and not to the glory of any mortal controversy.
We would live, not by a solitary phase of human
thought, but by every word of God that our ears
may be blessed to hear. We do not assemble to

* Cross St. Chapel, Manchester, where these sermons were
preached, is an old English Presbyterian Chapel, with an open
trust.

sharpen lines of distinction between ourselves and others, to the invariable disadvantage of the latter, but, in the hush of earthly passion and pursuit, to listen to the still voice which comes as a breathing of peace, with its own message of love, to each waiting heart. And therefore all who would come may come. Our invitation is, Come and drink of the waters of life freely. We ask you not your creed; we assume no lordship over either thought or conscience; you are a soul thirsting after God—it is sufficient; come, brother, and mingle your prayers with ours.

I know that these are often regarded as fine-spun thoughts, which are easily brushed away by the plain sense of mankind, just as Christianity seemed to the amiable and accomplished Gallio a mere 'question of words and names.' Men who differ dogmatically, it is magisterially asserted, never will worship together; the inference is generally left to be supplied—therefore we must take care that they never shall. Now I at once admit that there is a connection between our belief and our worship, and that this connection may be of such a kind as to make it impossible for certain classes of believers habitually to worship together. The Unitarian, however deep may be his appreciation of the feminine character, cannot join in worshipping the Virgin; and one who, however wide his charity, believes it indispensable to his religious life to worship the Virgin, could not for the sake of visible fellowship consent always to forego that part of his devotions. A similar remark would apply to the worship of Christ; and, to go a step further, a Jew could not easily join in our ordinary worship, so strongly tinged as it is with elements of Christian thought and feeling; nor, on the other hand, could we always bridle our lips and stay the outpourings of our hearts' gratitude for the gift of Jesus Christ. There will, therefore, probably always remain a sort of general and vague concurrence of opinion at any given time amongst the members of the same congregation. But there are two ways of dealing with this fact. One is, to insist on defining the concurrence which is necessary, and to impose it as a condition, either in the form of a creed or of a dogmatic name, upon the necks of the worshippers. This is the principle of exclusion, which, in proportion to its strictness, destroys the very roots of worship, because it always tends to limit our sense of religious brotherhood, and to exalt the form above the spirit. The other mode is to avoid all artificial restraints, to allow worship to find its own affinities, and leave it to the conscience of each worshipper to settle what is indispensable for him. This principle, though it may never bring Unitarians and Catholics into the same temple, will yet enable the Unitarian who accepts it to recognise in the devout Catholic a brotherly relation, which the Catholic, bound by terms of communion, cannot recognise in him; and it will gather into the same congregation larger and more varied elements of thought than would be possible under any other condition.

But, it is alleged, under such circumstances the pulpit is fettered, a man may not speak his own opinions. and preaching degenerates into pretty platitudes. I should say, on the contrary, that the pulpit is for the first time emancipated. The distinguishing characteristic of our pulpit is that the preachers who occupy it are expected to preach their own opinions, and not the opinions of some one else. In speaking all that is in their hearts, they are in no fear of violating any pledge, or denying a dogma which they were hired to support; nay, the only way in which they can violate the solemn pledge which they have taken on themselves before God, is by paying deference to party expectation, and holding back some truth which they think it would be good for you to hear. One thing, however, which may seem a restraint to the carnal man, is secured by the principle which has always marked our congregational life; and that is, that our preachers will treat religious questions in a large, scientific spirit, that they will show to others the same generous appreciation of conscientious belief which they expect others to show to them, and that thus they will raise the discussion of the most controverted points above the miserable squabbles of irreligious faction. Nothing so

removes the sting from our arguments as the knowledge that our words will be listened to by fellow-
worshippers of the most varying shades of opinion,
and that any flippant or party treatment of a subject
is sure to wound the tender reverence of some
brother's heart.   Thus the free principle secures at
once the most explicit and fearless statement of conviction, and the broadest catholicity in the pursuit
and the exposition of truth.

Brethren, is this freedom a grand inheritance or
not?   Is it 'a question of words and names,' or a
question between the eternal life of the invisible
Universal Church and the transient life of a little
sect?   To me it seems the very principle which all
that is noblest in the present age is feeling after, but
cannot yet express; and on us rests the glorious
responsibility of bearing a faithful testimony to its
truth and power.   But we shall be misunderstood,
and pursue a phantom!   Let us do our duty, and
leave our public estimation and our practical success
in the hands of God.   If this principle be true, men
might crucify us; but from our graves the tree
of life and liberty would grow, and flower with
immortal bloom.   Christ was misunderstood.   Christ's
views were Utopian.   Had he consulted more
deferentially the wisdom of the day, he probably
would not have been crucified.   But he insisted on
including the Samaritan in the Kingdom of God,
though everybody knew that the Samaritan would

not come. He insisted on taking in east and west, and north and south, though every one knew that his historical connection was with Judaism, that he was most unlikely to influence any but Jews, and that it seemed ungracious not to recognise by a limiting name the course of historical development. And so this seer of great visions, this prophet of an ideal kingdom, this dreamer that the hour was already come when men would worship the Father in spirit and in truth, was hunted to the cross amidst the derision of religionists and statesmen. Let us learn from this example; for the burden of the same truth rests upon our hearts to-day. But the kingdom is nearer than when Christ prayed and wept. Let us take his cross, and, at once abnegating self and refusing the compromises of a worldly policy, let us labour in faith and hope for that kingdom where men live by every word that proceedeth out of the mouth of God, where the spirit of worship rises above the separations of human narrowness, and where there is one brotherhood as there is one God and Father of all, who is above all, and through all, and in all!

XXII.

PARTING WORDS.

A Farewell Sermon, preached December 19. 1869.

1 Corinthians iii. 16.

*' Know ye not that ye are the temple of God, and that
the Spirit of God dwelleth in you ?'*

IF we would sum up in the briefest possible expression, and exhibit in its most universal form,
the substance of Christian faith and the central
thought of Christian teaching, we could hardly find
more suitable words than those contained in our
text. Under the leading of Christ, man was no
longer to seek for God through superstitious ceremonies, or in places marked off from the profane
world by an exclusive sanctity, but in his own heart,
cleansed and hallowed for a temple of the Divine
Spirit. Won by the reconciling Love which spoke
from the cross with mingled remonstrance and
appeal, he was to recognise God as a Father—not
only the Creator and Judge, but the indwelling
Spirit—who enriched the soul from the fulness of
his own life, breathed his restoring sympathy on the

repentant heart, and inspired each struggling aspiration towards a higher goodness and truth. Salvation
was to be sought, not through the propitiating bribe
of an expensive sacrifice, nor through the mediation
of a priestly order supposed to be influential with
Heaven, but through faith in God, a trustful offering
up of the will, a lowly resting in Him with the
blessed dependence of a Son.

From this leading thought we may gather the
nature of that worship which, at stated times, we have
endeavoured to offer here, and which flows spontaneously, when ' it listeth,' from minds in which
Christian thought has passed into Christian faith.

There is, first, the adoration of dependent creatures.
Under this term may be included all those feelings
of awe, reverence, wonder, admiration, which arise
towards One who is felt to be infinitely stronger,
wiser, and holier than we, and whose Being ascends
into heights and goes down into depths whither
human imagination strains itself in vain to follow.
It is no part of the most spiritual religion to forget
the transcendent and unapproachable greatness of
God, or to fling off that awe-inspiring sense of
mystery which has ever blended itself with man's
devoutest moods, and which must press upon every
mind that has not learned with vulgar inconsiderateness to confound the common with the unclean.
' Perfect love casts out *fear* ;' but it does not cast
out the solemnity of conscious dependence, or that

humbling conviction of our own ignorance, sinfulness, and ingratitude which forces itself upon us when we own, as we ought, the presence of a knowledge which is wider than the heavens, a sanctity which is purer than noonday light, and a tender kindness which interpenetrates all created things, providing for the stability of a universe, and condescending to paint the flower and to feed the worm.

Yet Christian worship would not be complete, if it stopped short with that veneration which might be felt towards a distant Ruler whose greatness bore no relation to ourselves ; it must pass on to communion—that fellowship of a child with a Father which adds to veneration a deeper intelligence, and changes its terror into trust. The soul would not only lift eyes of wonder to the unknown immensity, or cast a trembling look into the unfathomable abyss, but bathe itself in ' the life of God,' and become ' partaker of the Divine nature.' It would feel the throb of an immortal power within, and with quickened sense of responsibility, with higher view of the objects of human life, and with humbler acceptance of its conditions, would own itself a sanctuary of God.

We may conveniently notice this communion under three aspects.

We would seek communion with God in the possession of truth. This communion already exists in our native capacity for knowledge, and in those intellectual laws which, whatever account we may

give of their genesis, manifest themselves in all
rational beings with whom we are acquainted.
Under the guidance of this capacity and these laws,
we gradually accumulate knowledge, and gather our
various isolated judgments into the harmony of
wisdom, and thus attain, in some low degree, to
fellowship with the Divine thought. Now the thirst
for truth, and especially for moral and spiritual
truth, enters largely into our worship ; and although
there is no reason to suppose that dogmatic infallibility is guaranteed by the fervour of our prayer for
it, or that knowledge can be obtained except by the
slow process of faithful study, yet the lifting up of
the soul to Him who is true brings us to that single-
minded love of truth, that candid readiness to admit
an error and to abandon a prejudice, and that
humility and patience of research, which are the
indispensable conditions of larger knowledge and
deeper wisdom. And in regard to the higher
regions of thought, we find in worship alone some
of the fundamental data on which to build a true
science of duty and of God. The man who endeavours to live, as it were, outside of God, and never
seeks that nearer communion which belongs to
prayer, may speculate in vain upon the mysteries of
the Spirit. He knows nothing of the inward facts
which are clear to the devout, nor has he the loving
aspiration and self-forgetting simplicity to which
alone Truth will reveal her face. Therefore it is that

T

in worship we see and understand more fully the
Divine side of nature and of life, accepted truths are
borne to the soul laden with richer meaning and sug-
gestiveness, and we gain those flashes of spiritual
insight which never visit our colder and more worldly
moods. A ray from the infinite Intelligence shines
amid the darkness of our minds; and as it glows in
brighter beams, we exclaim, ' How precious are thy
thoughts unto us, O God! how great is the sum of
them!'

Again, we would seek communion with God in
spiritual beauty of character. ' Be ye holy, for I am
holy,' is a message intelligible only to those who
are conscious of some affinity with the Divine in the
region of the sentiments and emotions. This part
of our nature may be—alas! often is—chaotic and
stormy; yet it may, like an unruffled sea, reflect the
serene order of Heaven. There is a purity of thought,
a still depth of hallowed feeling, a subdued and
chaste power of strong emotion, a far-reaching
insight of compassionate sympathy, a self-renouncing
simplicity of love, which we must own to be nearer
to the Holy Spirit than the confused fierceness of
unchecked passion or the weary discontent of our
selfishness and greed. Into those highest sentiments
and purest graces of which our nature is susceptible
we would enter through the humility of worship:
and it is here pre-eminently that the communion of
prayer is needed and its kindling power felt. Our

emotions respond not to the command of the will, and are in no sense a creation of our own; for they precede our voluntary effort, and furnish the problems in which our activity must be engaged. If none but the meaner passions ever found entrance into our hearts, a life grand in its actions and effects would be impossible for us. The will can only work within the limits of divinely appointed conditions; and if the spontaneous life of the soul be remote from God, our most faithful efforts will achieve only a commonplace result. Hence our need of what have been called 'means of grace'—those various helps which experience shows to be capable of touching the deeper springs of sentiment, and exalting our emotional life into the peace and beauty of holiness. Chief among these is prayer. In the solemn hour when worship is offered in spirit and in truth, when eye and ear are closed against the world, and the meaner passions sleep under the lulling breath of devotion, we see 'visions and revelations of the Lord,' and hear a Word diviner far than we noticed amid the distraction of lower interests and cares. It is then that the soul experiences what it is to be a child of God; the problems to which our activity must be addressed are lifted to a higher sphere; and life's noblest possibilities are offered to our choice.

It remains, however, for ourselves to take up the burden of responsibility which is thus laid upon us;

and we must seek communion with God in righteousness, understanding by that word the voluntary
acceptance and practical carrying out of the best
course which is open to our choice. Here we touch
the department of human liberty, and recognise in
man an original agent, limited indeed in the direction of his efforts, but capable of choice among conflicting motives, and accountable for the exercise of
his active power. Sharers, under whatever restric-
tions and in however narrow a field, of the Divine
freedom, we reach here for the first time the
possibility of virtue, and become aware of the sad
reality of sin. We may direct our activity to unworthy ends, and use with selfish cupidity the
faculties which God has given us that we may work
out his purposes, not with the unintelligent instinct
of inferior creatures, but with the clear-eyed self-
renunciation of Sons. Man alone is capable at once
of knowing the Divine Will and saying, ' I won't
fulfil it ; ' but, when he so speaks, he abdicates the
position of a Son, and allies himself rather with satanic power. We must be ' labourers together with
God,' and bend our energies to the accomplishment
of our Father's Will. We must seek communion
with Him in the consecration of our active life, and
through word and deed manifest the Spirit of Him by
whom we live. Worship is of no avail, if the will
stand sullenly aloof, making reservations on behalf
of self, and seeking all the blessedness of religion

while contriving to evade its cross. First must be offered the sacrifice of the will, and each day's labour humbly dedicated ; and then the Father will come and make his abode with us, and sanctify us as temples of his Spirit.

Such then, in faintest sketch, is the nature of that worship which, as a Christian Church, we would offer to our God.

From this we may gather a few thoughts as to the nature and duties of a Church. Ought not a Church, composed as it is of many members, to possess a larger life than that of any individual, and to be in a fuller sense the temple of God? Ought it not to enshrine all those high qualities which we speak of as Divine, and to offer with wider meaning than the lonely heart can do that worship of adoration and communion which becomes the children of the Infinite Father? Ought it not to own its dependence with greater devoutness, to utter a broader truth and a deeper wisdom, to exhibit a purer sanctity, and to dedicate itself to the fulfilment of the Divine Will with a more complete self-abnegation, than belong to the smaller life of any single mind? Not only does it enjoy the advantage of the diverse gifts of its members, which supplement one another's deficiencies, but it is an association of men, not at their common level, but in their highest attitude of mind, and speaking, not the maxims which they too often follow, but the dictates of conscience and reason when purified by the influence of worship. The Church, therefore, though composed of men living in the world, ought to be above the world. The world consists of men manifesting the average wisdom and morals of the day; the Church, of the same men seeking after God, and setting forth, not the actual meanness, but the ideal glory of life. It is in this way that the Church is greater and wiser than any of us who yet help to compose it, and becomes to us a spiritual mother, from whose wisdom we may learn, with whose devotion we may be fired, with whose sympathy we may be consoled, by whose faith we may be quickened. A Church which knows that it is 'the temple of God' will thus, with loving care, foster the life of its members; and through the diversity of its gifts and operations, all working harmoniously together towards the good of the whole community, prove that the Spirit of God dwells within it.

Yet it is not the office of the Church to restrain, but only to enlarge, the individual life. It is essential to its own completeness freely to admit even what might seem the eccentricities of individual genius, and to make amplest provision for the original development of each of its members. It must not forget that its own wisdom is but the collective expression of those truths which have been delivered to the souls of men, one by one; and that in silencing the voice of any humble and

thoughtful man, it may be dishonouring that very
Spirit whose Word it professes to enshrine. It
imparts, therefore, along with its corporate life, the
fullest liberty which individualism can claim, sanctifying freedom as an expression, no longer of self-
will, but of the soul's right and duty to listen for
itself to those oracles of truth which surely are not
dumb in any temple of God. It is the duty of the
Church, not to check the luxuriance of individual
growth, but to smooth away the asperities of individual narrowness, and with its own broad and
loving wisdom enrich the solitary soul with that
fulness of life which comes from religious fellowship.
Each of its members ought to grow to the stature of
Christ, and to become himself a temple ; no partial
fane dedicated to some idol of human intolerance or
party zeal, but ' filled with all the fulness of God !'

Thus, then, our Christian worship, and our connection with a Christian Church, ought to lead us
to ' the life of God '—that life which alone is eternal,
which was and ever is with the Father, and was
manifested to us in Christ. The life of the Church
ought to be the continuation of the Saviour's life,
and each thirsting soul ought to be able to drink
from its deep wells and be satisfied. From the
Church ought to sound forth a perpetual appeal
to the mass of men. It ought to tend the sick in
body and in spirit ; to bind up the broken-hearted ;
to preach glad tidings to the poor ; to exhibit the

Divine sorrow for sin, and bring to the estranged
soul the peace of reconciling Mercy; and by the
serene majesty of its love, and the lowly faithfulness of its service, bear constant witness to a higher
world, and prove itself the temple of God. The
ideal is a lofty one, and most imperfectly is it
embodied in existing Churches. You may say that
it is higher than we can hope to attain; yet it is
well to read the Divine thought concerning us, and
to recognise in the light of God the full grandeur
of our calling. This will at once give the true
direction to our efforts, and clothe us in that humility which is the prime condition of all spiritual
graces. Oh, that this house of prayer, consecrated
as it is to a free worship, and welcoming the diverse
tendencies of a manifold life, may gather within its
walls a Church of the faithful, 'sons and daughters
of the Lord Almighty,' and prove in the future
more than in the past a sanctuary of peace and
hope, of truth and holiness, of duty and of love !

Time would forbid me to speak of the various
agencies through which the life of a Church may
manifest itself; but it may not be out of place to
allude for a moment to the special sphere of labour
which for ten years I have helped to fill among
you. From the general thought of this discourse
we may readily infer the duty of the Christian
minister. The *ideal* minister ought to combine
within himself all those great qualities which con-

stitute the truest life of the Church, and to possess
them in such fulness as to be capable of giving of
his abundance to others. His it is to unfold the
contents of the life of God within the soul, and give
to each spiritual fact its right interpretation and
position. On him it devolves to bring impressively
before the mind its dependence on the Infinite
Creator, to bow the sluggish soul in adoration, to
waken the drowsy conscience, and draw the tear of
penitence from the sinful. He has to speak the
word of comfort to the sorrowing, and show the
peace of Heaven to the dying. He has to appeal
to the simple and untrained intelligence of the child,
and to the strong thought and high resolve of the
earnest and cultured man. He has to meet the
wants of those who in life's battle would gain each
week a higher strength, and to lead their thoughts
to what is true, their sentiments to what is holy,
their activity to what is just and loving. And with
all this, he ought to be simplest in character, purest
in heart, most disinterested in purpose, lowliest in
personal claim—as willing, if need were, to wash the
feet of the poorest as to share the hospitality of the
rich. In a word, it ought not to be he that lived
among his people, but Christ that lived in him.

With such an ideal, one almost wonders at the
presumption which can undertake so great an office.
But it is not for us, when once the design of Providence is clear to our conviction, to measure our

own powers, but humbly to accept, with all our sins and deficiencies, the work which God assigns us. ' Our treasure is in earthen vessels, that the excellency of the power may be of God, and not of us.' It is He that lights the ideal before our thought, and keeps it so far above us that pride may not come in and spoil our efforts. Following with such faltering steps, and with such inconstant will, the Divine leading, we can only give thanks to God for whatever good we may achieve, and implore his pardon for the ill. And when any one with any loftiness of purpose looks back on an attempt to realise the dream of his boyhood, and the aspirations which the mercy of Heaven had kindled in his heart, he can only rest in the long-suffering love of his Father, and own how ' blessed is he whose transgression is forgiven, whose sin is covered.' But forgetting the failures of the past, and retaining only the humility and wisdom which they may have taught, let us look hopefully to the future, and commit ourselves in trust to each new task which God appoints us, believing that He who has led us hitherto will lead us still !

And now, brethren, beloved in the Lord, may the peace of God abide in all our hearts, and may that Father who will never leave us nor forsake us, help us in life and in death to glorify his name !

Spottiswoode & Co., Printers, New-street Square, London.

www.ingramcontent.com/pod-product-compliance
Lightning Source LLC
Chambersburg PA
CBHW031952060726
47497CB00016B/1470